Pasta G...

Step by Step Guide to

Easy and Delicious Italian

Pasta Recipes to Impress Your

Friends And Family

Introduction

Italy has a vast array of culinary masterpieces.

Such a broad palette of colors, which are different in every single geographic area, and within each geographic area, differing by individual territory, and in each individual city. It is truly the destination of the new Grand Tour, which now not only seeks beauty in archaeology, architecture, art, or landscapes, but also in time-honored delicacies with a modern heart. Here, history, climate, environment, manual dexterity, and culinary genius have merged, and continue to blend into an inimitable harmony.
Artichoke salad with Parmigiano-Reggiano cheese; Penne All'Arrabbiata; Branzino All'Acqua Pazza; mixed fish fry; capon stuffed with chestnuts; asparagus with Parmigiano-Reggiano cheese;
Baci di Dama with cacao; peaches with amaretti; zabaglione.

This is a mere glimpse of a possible gastronomic itinerary along the Italian peninsula, and the list goes on. It is estimated that in Italy there are over 3000 typical dishes, just counting the fundamental ones. There are many more, if we take into account the numerous creative variants that each recipe has carried along with itself over time. While being quite aware of having left out many others, we have collected those considered the best—for quality, truth, and wisdom—for rais-ing awareness of the primacy of Italian cuisine. In these recipes, respect for the territory—seen not only as a physical space, but also social and cul-tural—and investment into the legacy of the past have come together, with a pinch of poetry and innovation. not only the typical dishes have been consecrated by tradition, but also the creations that are typically Italian for their successful alchemy of gastronomic intuition, executive ability, and use of great products typical of the Bel Paese. Examples include buffalo mozzarella from Campania,Pecori no Romano, radicchio di Treviso, Taggiasca olives, balsamic vinegar of Modena, Sicilian pistachios, and Piedmontese hazelnuts. And in the culinary universe of the peninsula, even though there are dishes with considerable complexity, the overwhelming majority are characterized by the elegance of simplicity: They require just a few ingredients of very high quality, and the creativity and care to bring out their best in just a few steps.

Perhaps this is because the majority of the jewels of Italian cuisine—which also include many recipes of aristocratic ancestry—come from dishes with a humble origin, and were born making use of inexpensive, everyday ingredients, yet filled with imagination and flavor. For example, classic Vermicelli with Tomato Sauce has exquisite originality because of its very simplicity. Such recipes have turned necessity into a virtue. These are simple preparations, but were quickly admitted into the most esteemed dining halls, and have now risen to the ranks of refined specialties.

Some of them can boast service for centuries, if not millennia. Just think of the traditional cream of fava beans. Even the ancient Romans had a passion for this legume, as proven by their many recipes still used on the peninsula today. Other dishes are more recent, yet have already entered into the Olympus of the most representative recipes of Italy. The gourmet Tiramisu, for example, one of the most well-known spoon desserts, was born in a restaurant in Treviso, in the Veneto region, in the late 1960s.

The fame of Italian cuisine, however, depends not only upon the delicacy of the dishes themselves, prepared with skill and with quality products, but also upon the way it expresses the significance of a good life. The food is a metaphor for a lifestyle that is typically Italian: sunny, open, creative, and joyful, where good humor gives you an appetite, and vice versa. And this philosophy— an outlook on the kitchen, but also on the world—is something that all Italians have in common

INTRODUCTION 3
- Garden Pasta 9
- Garlic Parmesan Pasta 11
- Garlicky Beef and Pasta 13
- GrandMom's Pasta 15
- Grilled Shrimp With Pasta and Fresh Tomatoes 16
- Hogan's Ultimate Pasta Salad 18
- Hot Tuna & Pasta Salad 20
- Italian Brochettes with Angel Hair Pasta 22
- Italian Meat Pasta Sauce 24
- Lemon Tuna Pasta 26
- Lone Star Steak and Pasta 27
- Mamma's Pasta e Fagioli 29
- Mandarin-Style Pasta 31
- Manestra (Pasta) 33
- Pasta salad with avocado 35
- Pasta Salad with Chicken and Artichokes 37
- Pasta Shells with Lemon Vinaigrette 38
- Pasta Stew with Rosemary Pork 40
- Market Pasta Salad 43
- Mexicali Pasta Salad 45
- Mexican Pasta Pie 46
- One Pot Tuna Pasta 48
- Pasta 50
- Pasta - Basic Recipe for Homemade 52
- Pasta & Bean Soup 54
- Pasta & Strawberries Romanoff 56
- Pasta Al Forno 58
- Pasta Al Pesto 60
- Pasta Ala Oglio with Shrimp 62
- Pasta ala Puttanesca 64
- Pasta and Smoked Salmon Salad 66
- Pasta Carbonara 68
- Pasta Chowder 70
- Pasta Di Pina 72
- Pasta E Fagiole Soup for Crockpot 74
- Pasta E Fagioli 76
- Pasta Flora, Athens Style 78
- Pasta Green Salad 80
- Pasta in Cream Sauce w/Poultry Magic 82
- Pasta Marco Polo 84

Pasta Primavera 85
Pasta Primavera Special 87
Pasta Salad 89
CONCLUSION 91

Garden Pasta

5	Tomatoes, chopped	1/4	tsp	Garlic powder
2	Celery, chopped	1/2	tsp	Salt
2	Carrots, chopped	1/2	tsp	Pepper
1	Onion, medium, chopped	1/2	tsp	Oregano
8	Green onion, chopped	1	Tbs	Vegetable or salad oil
1	package Equal	1	lb	Spaghetti
1 tsp	Basil			

Procedure

1 Put the vegetables in a pot and cover tightly. Cook over medium heat, stirring occasionally, for 10 min. Add seasonings. Cover pot, cook medium-low heat for 5 minutes. Add oil and simmer for 30 min. or until carrots are tender. Cook spaghetti, drain. Toss with the sauce. Cal: 150; Fat: 1/2g.

Servings: 6

Garlic Parmesan Pasta

1/2	cup	Butter Or Margarine	8	oz	Fettuccine; Cooked & Drained
2	tsp	Dried Basil; Crushed			
2	tsp	Lemon Juice	1 1/2	cup	Broccoli Floweretts; Cooked Tender Crisp
1 1/4	tsp	Garlic Powder W/Parsley			
3/4	tsp	Seasoned Salt	3	Tbs	Walnuts; Chopped
			1/2	cup	Parmesan Or Romano Cheese Grated

Procedure

1. Melt the butter in a large skillet and add the basil, lemon juice, garlic powder and seasoned salt, blending well. Add the fettuccine, broccoli, walnuts and parmesan cheese, blending well and tossing to coat the fettuccine.
2. PRESENTATION:
3. Serve with a fresh spinach salad.

Servings: 4

Garlicky Beef and Pasta

1 1/2	cup	Uncooked rotoni pasta (Spirals)	1/8	tsp	Pepper (or 1/4 ts)
1	lb	Beef round tip steak, cut 1/8 to 1/4 inch thick	1	Tbs	Water
		Vegetable cooking spray	2	cup	Frozen cut green beans about 8 ounces
2		Cloves garlic, crushed	1/2	cup	Jarred brown beef gravy
1/2	tsp	Salt			

Procedure

1. Cook pasta according to package directions; keep warm. Meanwhile stack beef steaks; cut lengthwise in half and then crosswise into -inch-wide strips.
2. Spray large non-stick skillet with cooking spray; place skillet over medium-high heat until hot. Add beef and garlic, half at a time, and stir-fry 1 minute or until outside surface of beef is no longer pink. Don't overcook. Season with salt and pepper. Remove from skillet; keep warm. In same skillet, heat water until hot. Add green beans; cook 4 or 5 minutes or until tender, stirring occasionally. Stir in gravy and pasta; heat through. Return beef to skillet; toss to combine.
3. Approximate values per serving: 296 calories, 7 g fat, 70 mg cholesterol, 488 mg sodium, 21 percent calories from fat.

Servings: 4

GrandMom's Pasta

10	oz	Italian sausage				Or any pasta sauce
2	tsp	Water		1/4	cup	Heavy cream
1		Jar Pasta Sauce with basil and garlic		1	lb	Rigatoni, cooked Fresh grated Parmesan cheese

Procedure

1. Remove sausage from casing and crumble into a large saucepot. Add the water and cook over low heat for 20 minutes, or until it is cooked. Drain off fat. Add pasta sauce and simmer for 5 minutes. Stir in cream.
2. Serve pasta sauce over cooked rigatoni and top with cheese.
3.

Servings: 6

Grilled Shrimp With Pasta and Fresh Tomatoes

1	lb	large shrimp	1	tsp	Dijon mustard
3/4	cup	fruity olive oil	4		large ripe tomatoes, cut into chunks
		salt and fresh black pepper			
3	Tbs	balsamic vinegar	20		leaves fresh basil, roughly chopped
1		shallot minced			
			1	lb	penne

Procedure

1 Set a large pot of salted water to boil for the pasta; start a charcoal fire or light a gas grill. Brush the shrimp with about 1/4 c olive oil; sprinkle them with salt and pepper. mix together the remaining olive oil, 2 TB of the vinegar, the shallot, and mustard, and season with salt and pepper. taste to add more vinegar if needed. set the tomatoes in a large bowl to marinade with the vinaigrette and basil. Grill the shrimp over high heat until they turn pink, about 2-3 minutes per side; meanwhile, cook the pasta according to the package directions. Drain the pasta, toss with the tomatoes, top with the grilled shrimp, and serve.

2 Crawfish works great with this dish also.

Servings: 4

Recipe Type

Bbq List, Fish And Seafood

Hogan's Ultimate Pasta Salad

		=== SALAD ===	1	Tbs	Salad oil
16	oz	Three Spiral Pasta			=== DRESSING ===
8	oz	Tortellini, cheese-filled	1	Tbs	Salad oil
1/2	cup	Parmesan cheese, grated	3	Tbs	Red wine vinegar
1/2	cup	Cheddar cheese, grated	2	Tbs	Dijon mustard
1/8	cup	Black olives, chopped	1	Tbs	Lemon juice
1/8	cup	Carrots, shredded	1	cup	Mayonnaise
3/4	cup	Bell pepper, diced	1	Tbs	Garlic, fresh, minced
1	cup	Peas	1	Tbs	Basil, fresh, minced
3/4	cup	Red onion, diced	1	Tbs	Oregano, fresh, minced
1 1/2	cup	Tomatoes, diced	3/4	tsp	Dry mustard for dressing
1/2	cup	Dill, fresh, chopped			Salt to taste for dressing
1	cup	Ham, cubed small			Pepper to taste for dressing
2		Eggs, hard-boiled			

Procedure

1. DIRECTIONS:
2. Boil pasta according to package directions; drain, then cool.
3. Heat salad oil in skillet and add the bell peppers and saute until just becoming tender.
4. Mix all other "salad" ingredients together, then add the sauteed bell peppers, also.
5. Prepare "dressing" then mix in with "salad".
6. Toss well, cover and chill.
7.

Servings: 12

Hot Tuna & Pasta Salad

1/2	cup	Mayonnaise	10	oz	Frozen Chopped Broccoli, thawed
1/4	cup	Lemon juice			
1	Tbs	Dijon Mustard	2	cup	Carrots, sliced and cooked
1		lg Salad White Tuna	2	tsp	Soy Sauce
1/2	lb	Mediuxm Shell Macaroni	1/8	tsp	Ginger
			1/8	tsp	Basil

Procedure

1 Cook pasta per directions. Cook broccoli per directions. Combine mayonnaise, lemon juice, mustard, soy sauce, ginger and basil in a bowl. Toss with hot macaroni, tuna, broccoli and carrots. Mix and serve warm.

2

Servings: 1

Italian Brochettes with Angel Hair Pasta

2		sm Japanese eggplants	1	pinch	Crushed red pepper
1		Zucchini			Grated zest of 1 lemon
1		Yellow crookneck squash	1/2	tsp	Salt, optional
1/2	lb	Button mushrooms	1/2	tsp	Pepper, optional
1		Red bell pepper	9		Garlic cloves
1		Yellow bell pepper			Juice of 2 lemons
2		sm Red onions	1/4	cup	Vegetable broth or olive oil
1		Fennel bulb			
1/2	lb	Cherry toamtoes			**PASTA**
		MARINADE	1/2	cup	Tomato sauce
1/2		bn Fresh thyme	1	lb	Angel hair pasta

Procedure

1. Cut eggplant, squash & zucchini into pieces 1/4" thick. Halve mushrooms & cut bell peppers into strips. Quarter removing skins only if they are dirty. Trim outer leaves of fennel & remove any dirt. Slice into 8 thin wedges. Place all vegetables into large bowl.
2. MARINADE: Strip thyme leaves from stems, reserve stems. In a processor, process thyme, red pepper, zest & salt & pepper. Add garlic while machine is running. Stop machine & add lemon juice Turn on & add vegetable broth in a slow stream. Process 1 minute. Pour over vegetables & allow to marinate for 15 minutes.
3. Preapre grill & cover to build intense heat. Skewer vegetables. Toss sthyme stems onto the heat shield or coals. Place brochettes onto hot grill, cover & allw to smoke for 5 minutes. Remove cover, turn & cook for another 3 to 5 minutes.
4. Meanwhile, drain marinade into a small non-reactive pot. Add tomato sauce & heat through. When skewers are almost done, cook pasta. Drain & return to pot. Pour sauce over pasta & toss to coat. Serve with grilled vegetables.
5. VARIATION: Use sourdough bread brushed with the marinade & lightly grilled instead of the pasta.
6. PER SERVING: 314 Cal.; 14g Prot.; 3g Fat; 58g Carb.; 0 Chol.; 240mg Sod.; 8g Fiber.

Servings: 6

Italian Meat Pasta Sauce

1	cup	Onion; chopped	6	oz	-water (optional)
1	lb	Ground beef; lean	2		Stalks celery with tops chopped
2		Garlic cloves; minced	2	tsp	Salt
2		cn Tomatoes (1 lb-12 oz. ea.)	1/2	tsp	MSG (optional)
1		cn Tomato paste (4 oz)	3	tsp	Oregano; crushed

Procedure

1 Put all ingredients in crockpot and stir thoroughly. Cover and cook on LOW for 10 to 18 hours. Serve over spaghetti. Sprinkle with parmesan cheese if desired. Garnish with chopped parsley.

Servings: 6

Lemon Tuna Pasta

4	tsp	Butter	18		Black olives, pitted & sliced
1	tsp	Oil; olive	2	cn	Tuna; chunk, drained
4		lg Garlic cloves, chopped			Pasta; penne, cooked and dr
1/8	cup	Lemon juice	4	tsp	Butter (add at end)
3	tsp	Capers, drained			

Procedure

1 Melt butter with oil in skillet. Add garlic and cook 2 minutes. Add lemon juice, capers and olives and cook another 2 minutes. Turn heat to lowest setting. Add tuna & separate it (do NOT flake) with a fork. Heat through, stirring gently. Drain pasta. Add remainder of butter and sauce to hot pasta, tossing well.

Servings: 4

Lone Star Steak and Pasta

One of the National Pasta Association's Top 10 Favorites from the "Great States of Pasta" Recipe Contest Winners!

1	lb	Rotini or other medium pasta shape	1	cup	frozen corn, thawed and drained
1 1/4	lbs	boneless beef top sirloin steak, 1" thick	1/4	cup	green onion, sliced
1	Tbs	olive oil	1/2	cup	loosely packed cilantro leaves
1/4	cup	fresh lime juice	2	tsp	garlic, minced
1 10	oz	can diced tomatoes with green chilies, undrained	1/2	tsp	ground cumin
1 16	oz	can black beans, rinsed and drained	1	tsp	salt
1	cup	green pepper, chopped			

Procedure

1. Cook pasta according to package directions.
2. While pasta is cooking, trim fat from steak and cut lengthwise in half and then crosswise into 1/8" thick strips.
3. Heat oil in large nonstick skillet over medium-high heat. Add steak, half at a time and cook 1-2 minutes or until outside surface is no longer pink. Remove steak and set aside.
4. In same skillet, add lime juice, tomatoes and chilies, black beans, green pepper, corn, onion, cilantro, garlic, cumin, and salt. Cook and stir until hot. Add cooked meat and cook until heated through.
5. Serve with steak and vegetable mixture over pasta.

Servings: 6

Recipe Type

Main Dish, Pasta

Mamma's Pasta e Fagioli

16	oz	Can of cannellini beans	1/2	lb	Elbow or ditalini macaroni, Cooked al dente
8	oz	Can of tomato sauce			Fresh parsley, chopped
1	cup	Water			Grated cheese
2		Cloves of garlic, minced			
2	Tbs	Olive oil			

Procedure

1 Fry the garlic in oil gently until golden brown. Add the tomato sauce & water and cook for 10 minutes. Add the beans, stir gently. Drain and add the pasta to the bean mixture. Stir gently. If it gets too thick, add a little water. Add the parsley and serve immediately or the pasta will absorb all the liquid. Sprinkle with cheese and serve with Italian bread

Servings: 4

Mandarin-Style Pasta

1/2	cup	Hoisin sauce
3	Tbs	Low-salt soy sauce
3/4	cup	-ketchup
1/4	cup	Dry sherry
		Garlic clove, crushed
2	tsp	Sesame oil
1/3	cup	Green onion, sliced
1/8	tsp	-pepper
1 1/2	lb	Turkey breast slices, uncooked, cut into 1/4" X 1/2" X 1" strips
12	oz	Angel hair or fettucine pasta
		Sesame seeds, toasted

Procedure

1 In large bowl, combine hoisin sauce, soy sauce, ketchup, sherry, garlic, seasame oil, green onion and pepper. Stir in turkey strips. Pour into crockpot. Cover; cook on LOW 4 1/2 to 5 hours or until turkey is tender. Spoon over cooked pasta; toss. Sprinkle with sesame seeds. 1 serving contains: Cal 464; Prot 38g; Carb 60g; Fat g; Chol 66mg; sodium 1061mg.

Servings: 6

Manestra (Pasta)

6	cup	Lamb (or chicken) broth	16	oz	Tomato bits
16	oz	Manestra or rice	1/2	cup	Romano cheese; grated

Procedure

1 Combine lamb broth, manestra, and tomato bits; cook over medium heat for 20 minutes. Sprinkle with cheese, and serve.

Servings: 10

Pasta salad with avocado

1/2 x Avocado
x Tomatoes, diced 3/4 inch
2 cup Shell macaroni, cooked 1/4 cup Red onion, sliced

1   cn Water-packed albacore tuna, Drained
3 Tbs Bottled vinegar based dress.

Procedure

1 Cut avocado half into large 3/4 inch dices. Combine all ingredients and gently toss together.

Servings: 2

Pasta Salad with Chicken and Artichokes

Lb Pasta shells
Tbs Oil
1 1/2 cup Mayonnaise
3 Tbs Lemon juice
3 Tbs Chopped parsley

1 tsp Dried parsley
3 cup Diced cooked chicken
6 oz Jar artichokes chopped and
1 Dash of tabasco
1 Toasted almonds

Procedure

1 Cook pasta in large pot of boiling, salted water until tender, but firm, 8 to 12 minutes, stirring often. Drain well and rinse with cold water. Shake out excess water and toss pasta with oil. Combine mayonnaise, lemon juice, parsley and basil. Place pasta in large bowl. Add mayonnaise mixture, chicken, artichokes and tabasco. Toss well. Garnish with almonds. For a decorative presentation, serve in avacado halves, in tomato cups or on lettuce leaves. Yields 6-8 servings.

Servings: 6

Pasta Shells with Lemon Vinaigrette

12   x Jumbo Pasta Shells ---FILLING--- /2 c Ricotta cheese, part skim T Chopped fresh chives * /4 tBlack Pepper T Grated Lemon Peel /2 c Very finely chopped Almonds
-LEMON VINAIGRETTE- /4 c Lemon juice T Olive oil t Dijon Mustard T Chopped fresh parsley T Basil x Clove garlic, finely minced
* or 1 T dried chives or 1 chopped scallion

Procedure

1. GARNISH: Sliced almonds, cherry tomatoes, lemon wedges, fresh basil leaves or fresh parley sprigs, or sauteed pine nuts, and Parmesan cheese, optional. Bring a large pot of water to a boil; cook pasta until al dente. While pasta is cooking, combine FILLINGingredients in a med bowl. Set aside. In a large bowl, combine VINAIGRETTE ingredients. Set aside. When pasta is done, drain well, rinse under cold water, and drain well again. Toss shells with dressing to coat. Stuffshells with filling mixture, allowing 1 heaping Tablespoon for each. Arrange on serving platter. Drizzle each with some of the remaining dressing. Top with garnish(es) and serve immediately or chill. VARIATIONS: - substitute 6pieces of lasagna for pasta shells, spread each with filling, then roll up jelly- roll fashion - substitute 1/2 to 1 cup mashed tofu for part of ricotta cheese, or for all of ricotta if you're a real tofu fan - in place of Lemon Vinaigrette, use Herbed Tomato Sauce

Servings: 4

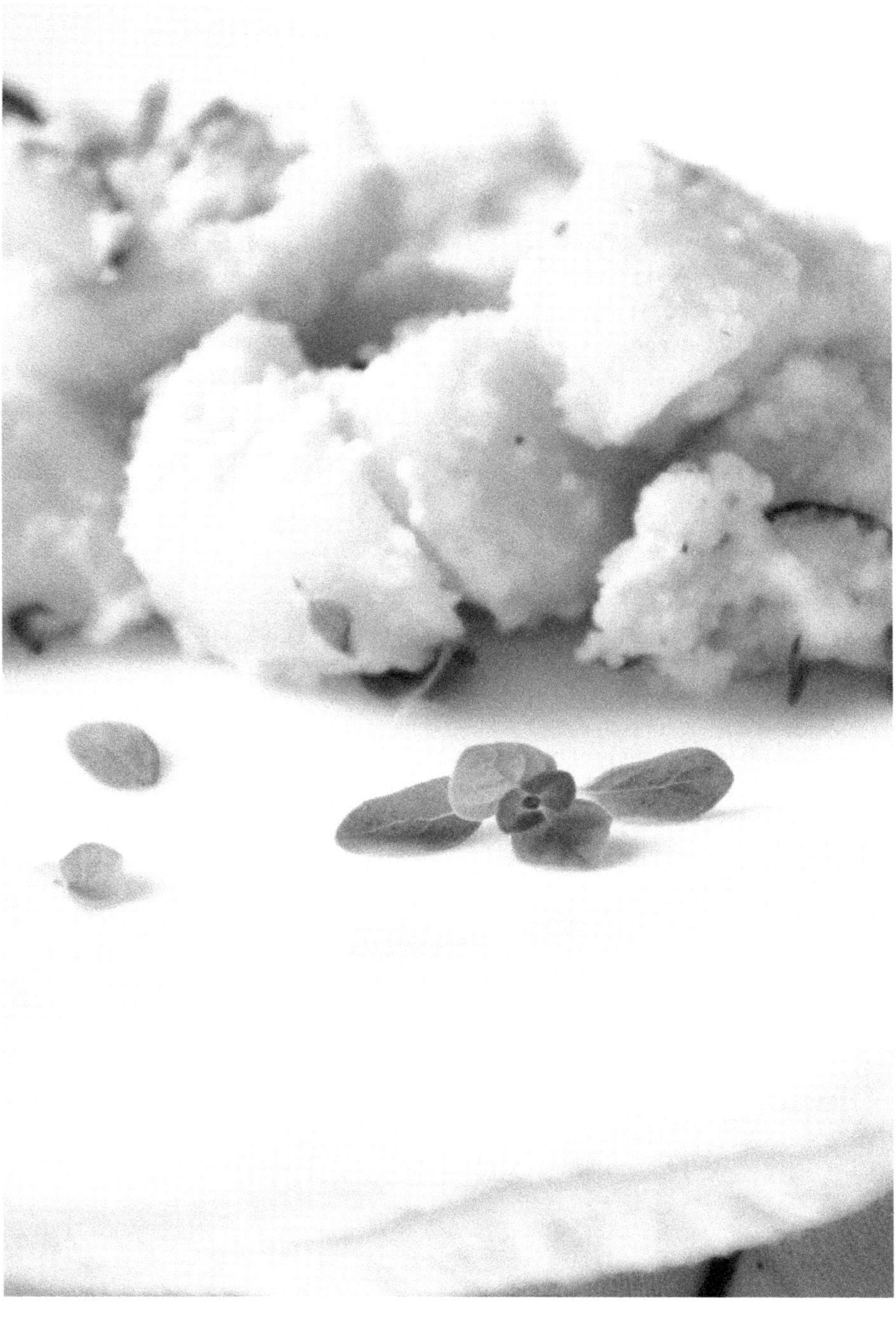

Pasta Stew with Rosemary Pork

8	oz	Ditalini, Orzo or Alphabets, uncooked	1 1/2	Tbs	minced fresh rosemary or 1 1/2 tsp. dried rosemary
1	tsp	vegetable oil	1/2	tsp	salt
1	lb	lean, boneless pork loin, cut into 3/4-inch cubes	2		medium sweet potatoes, peeled and cut into 1-inch cubes (about 3 cups)
1/8	tsp	ground red pepper			
1/8	tsp	black pepper	2	cups	chopped fresh spinach
1	cup	chopped onion	2	Tbs	lime juice
1/2	cup	chopped celery			
3		13 1/4-oz. cans fat-free, low-sodium beef broth			

Procedure

1. Heat oil in a large Dutch oven or pot until hot. Add pork; cook until no longer pink, about 4 to 5 minutes. Drain well. Toss pork with red and black pepper in a bowl; set aside.
2. Add 1/4 cup beef broth to pot; add onion and celery, and cook until tender. Add pork, remaining beef broth, rosemary and salt. Bring to a boil. Add pasta and sweet potatoes and boil, stirring occasionally, for 10 to 15 minutes or until pasta is done. Stir in spinach and lime juice. (Stew will continue to absorb liquid.) Serve immediately.

Servings: 6

Recipe Type

Main Dish, Meat, Pasta

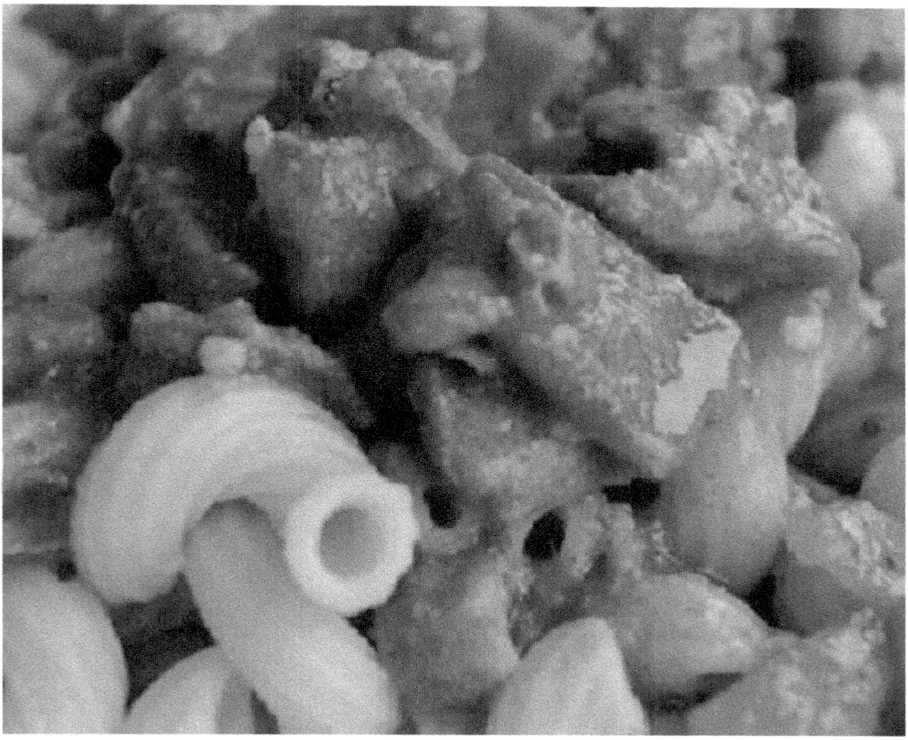

Market Pasta Salad

SALAD

8	oz	Shell macaroni, medium size uncooked
2	cup	Broccoli flowerets
1/2	cup	Onion, chopped (1 med.)
2	cup	Zucchini OR Yellow squash sliced 1/4 inch thick
1		Red pepper (med.) cut into strips
1	cup	Cheddar cheese (4 ounces) cut into 1/2 inch cubes

Procedure

1. ---DRESSING--- /2 c Vegetable oil /2 ts Salt /4 ts Pepper tb Lemon juice tb Dijon mustard ts Worcestershire sauce /2 ts Garlic, fresh, finely - chopped tb Parmesan cheese, freshly - grated
2. Cook macaroni according to package directions; drain. In a large bowl stir together all salad ingredients except cheese; stir in hot macaroni. Refrigerate 10 minutes. Stir in cheese. Meanwhile, in a medium bowl stir together all dressing ingredients except parmesan cheese. Pour dressing over salad, toss to coat. Sprinkle with parmesan cheese. Yield: 6 servings.
3. NUTRITION INFORMATION (1 Serving): Calories - 410 Protein - 12g Carbohydrate - 33g Fat - 26g Cholesterol - 22mg Sodium - 418mg

Servings: 6

Mexicali Pasta Salad

8	oz	Tri-color Pasta Spirals; *	1	Tbs	Cilantro; Fresh, Snipped
6		Tomatillos; Sm., **	2	Tbs	Vegetable Oil
1/2		Jalapeno Chile;	1/2	tsp	Lime Peel; Grated
20	oz	Pineapple Chunks;	1/4	tsp	Salt

Procedure

1 3 Cups of uncooked pasta should be used. ** Each tomatillo should be cut into 8 wedges. *** The jalapeno should be seeded and finely chopped. The pineapple chunks should be the ones canned in their own juice. Cook the pasta as directed on the package and drain. Rinse with cold water and drain again. Mix the pasta, tomatillos, chile and pineapple. Mix the reserved juice and the remaining ingredients. Pour over the pasta mixture and toss. Cover and refrigerate until chilled, at least 2 hours.

Servings: 6

Mexican Pasta Pie

1/2		Onion, finely chopped	2	Tbs	Olive oil
1	28 oz	Can tomatoes w/juice, - coarsely chopped	1 2	cup	Part-skim ricotta cheese (8-ounce) Chicken=boneless, - skinless breast halves
1		pk (1.25 oz) Taco seasoning mix			- cut in 1/2" pieces
1	16 oz	Can black beans, rinsed and - drained	1	cup	Shredded Cheddar or - Mexi-blend cheese
4	cup	Cooked ziti or penne pasta - (1 3/4 cup dried pasta)			

Procedure

1. (Leave out the chicken to convert to a vegetarian meal.)
2. Heat oven to 425 degrees. Grease a 7- x 11-inch baking dish.
3. In a medium nonreactive bowl, mix onions, tomatoes, taco mix and black beans. Toss pasta with olive oil.
4. Spread 1 cup tomato mixture on bottom of baking dish. Add cooked pasta. Dot with ricotta and then spread with a knife. Stir chicken pieces into remaining tomato mixture and spoon over ricotta. Sprinkle with shredded cheese. Bake 25 to 30 minutes. Serve immediately.

Servings: 6

Recipe Type

Pies

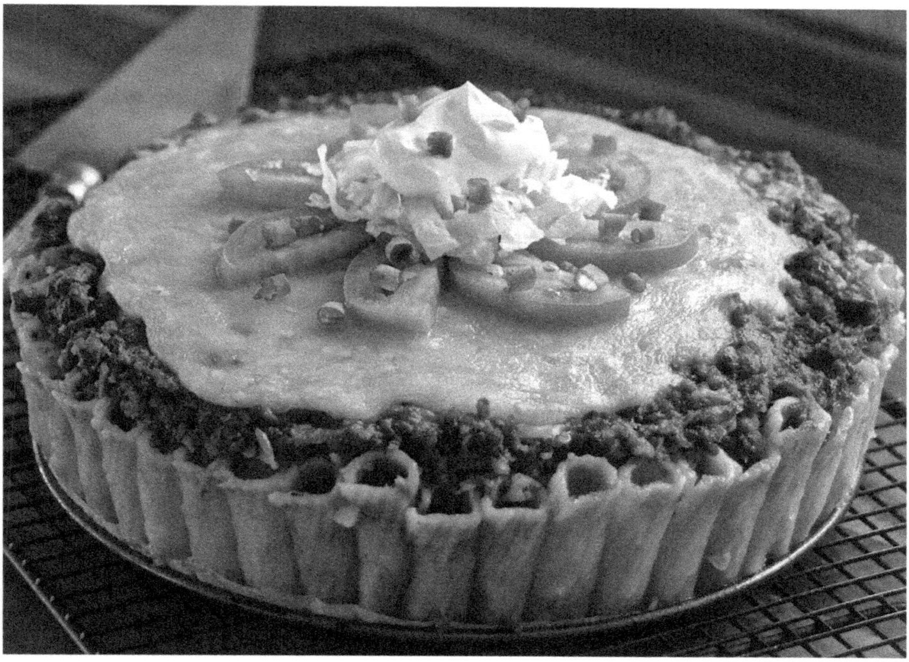

One Pot Tuna Pasta

8	oz	Elbow Macaroni, Medium Shells or other medium pasta shape, uncooked	1		9-oz. package frozen cut green beans
2 1/2	cups	water	1	cup	skim milk
2		chicken bouillon cubes	4	oz	low-fat Cheddar cheese, grated
1/8	tsp	black pepper	1		6 1/8-oz. can white albacore tuna packed in water, drained
1	tsp	fresh basil leaves			
1		4-oz. jar pimento	1/4	cup	chopped fresh parsley

Procedure

1. Bring water, bouillon cubes, pepper and basil leaves to a boil in a 4-quart pot. Gradually add pasta so that water continues to boil. Cover and simmer for 7 minutes, stirring occasionally.
2. Meanwhile, dice pimento. Stir diced pimento, green beans and milk into pot; cover and simmer 6 to 8 minutes or until pasta and beans are tender. Stir in cheese, tuna and parsley until cheese is melted.
3. Serve immediately.

Servings: 4

Recipe Type

Main Dish, Pasta

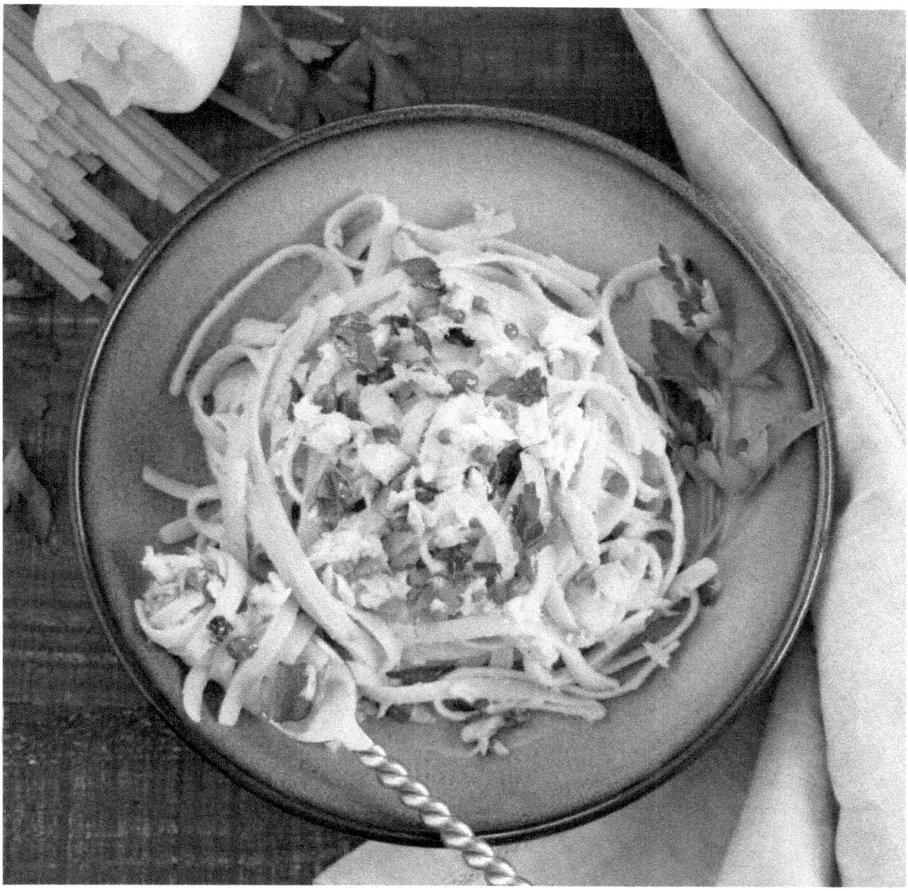

Pasta

3/4 lb	Rotini pasta	1	Yellow pepper, sweet
6	Green onions; sliced -OR-	10	Black olives; sliced
1/2	-Red onion; thin sliced	1/4 cup	Lemon juice; or vinegar
1	Red pepper, sweet	1/4 cup	Olive oil
1	Green pepper, sweet		

Procedure

1 In a large pot of boiling, salted water cook pasta til just tender. drain. Toss with onions, peppers, olives, lemon juice or vinegar, oil and salt and pepper to taste. SERVES: 5-6

Servings: 6

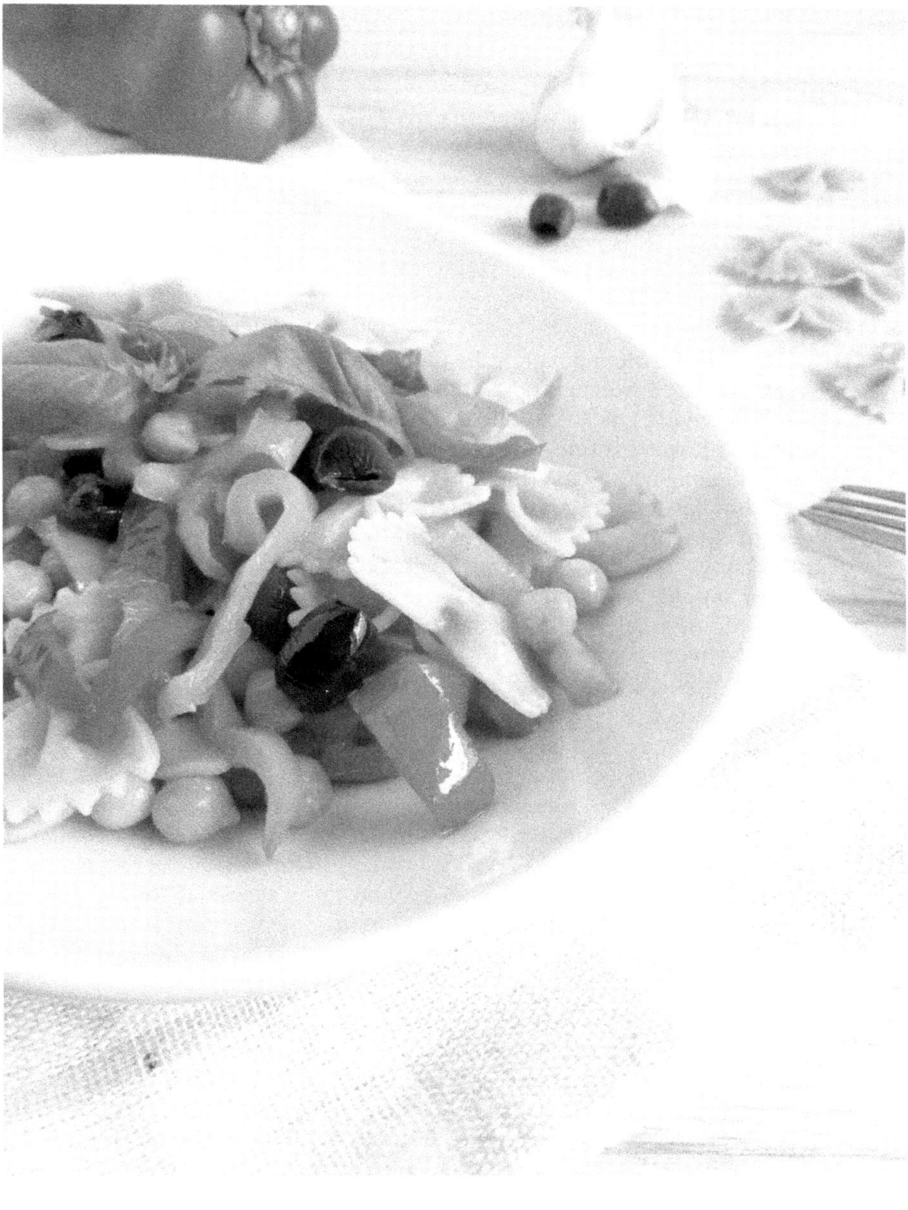

Pasta - Basic Recipe for Homemade

2 1/2 cup Flour;unbleached; up to 3 cups
4 Eggs;slightly beaten

Procedure

1. Ricetta Base Per Pasta in Casa (Basic Recipe for Homemade Pasta)
2. HAND ROLLED: Mound part of the flour in a large board or other working surface and make a well at center. Pour in eggs. With the aid of a fork, mix eggs and flour very gradually until a soft paste forms. With your finger mix in enough flour to make a firm but not too hard, dough. Knead for about 5 minutes, till dough is smooth. Place in an unfloured dish; cover with an inverted dish and let it rest in the refrigerator for about 1/2 hour. Take half of the dough, knead it lightly, and shape into a ball. Place on a well floured board. With the palms of your hands, flatten the ball, keeping the round shape, and sprinkle with flour. With the rolling pin, begin to thin the disk out in all directions, trying not to lose the round shape. Continue to sprinkle with flour as it becomes necessary, so that the dough does not stick to the pin. As soon as the disk of dough is thin enough to be rolled AROUND the rolling pin do so.* Starting from the end farthest from you, begin to roll the dough toward you, using small, even strokes back and forth, at the same time you swiftly slide your hands inward to the centre and outward to the edges of the pin. When the sheet is all rolled around the pin, PUSH the pin away from you at arm's length; then vigorously ROLL it back towards you, so that one side of the sheet flaps several times over the board. Turn the pin 90 degrees and unroll the sheet from it. Repeat from * as many times as needed for the desired thinness. Repeat with the other half of the dough and use as directed in each individual recipe. SERVES: 6 to 16, depending on the different uses made of it
3. WITH A HAND OPERATED MACHINE: Make a dough, using the method described above or by mixing eggs and flour in bowl. Knead over a well-floured board, mixing until they have a very firm dough. There is no need to make it smooth because the machine will take care of that. Place in an unfloured dish; cover with an inverted dish and let it rest in the refrigerator for about 1/2 hour. Take 1/4th of the dough at a time and begin the thinning. With the rollers set at the first slot (farthest apart), feed the dough between the rollers while turning the crank. If some of the dough sticks to the rollers or to

the machine, that means the dough is too soft and more flour must be added. Fold and feed with the rollers set at the same slot 3 or 4 times, until the sheet comes out in one piece (but not too smooth). Move on to the second slot and feed the sheet only once. Keeping on moving till the desired thinness is achieved. For lasagna or fettucini you stop at the next to last slot. For taglierini or calzonicchi, go through the last slot once, wait a few seconds, then feed the sheet into the last slot again. (Pasta made with only eggs and flour tends to be very elastic and it tends to shrink. However, the second time through it keeps the shape better.) Repeat with the remaining pasta, using 1/4th of the original quantity each time. Use as directed in the individual recipe.

4 *for electric pasta makers, follow the manufacturer's directions, but most machines will not provide sheet pasta for lasagna, ravoli, etc.
5 SERVES: 6 to 16, depending on the different uses made of it.

Servings: 1

Pasta & Bean Soup

1/2	cup	Elbow macaroni,shells, etc	15	oz	Can Chick Peas, drained *
2	Tbs	Safflower oil	16	oz	Can Kidney beans, drained *
		Med Onion, chopped			
		Clove Garlic, minced	3/4	tsp	Black pepper
1/2		x Green Bell Pepper, chopped	1/2	tsp	Summer savory
			1/2	tsp	Thyme leaves
3	cup	Vegetable stock or water	1	dash	Cayenne Pepper
6	oz	Can Tomato Paste (2/3 cup)			

Procedure

1 * rinsed well, then drained GARNISH: grated Parmesan cheese, optional
Cook pasta in boiling water for about 6 minutes, until al dente. While pasta is cooking, in Dutch oven or 4-5 qt saucepan, heat oil. Stir in onion, garlic, and green pepper. Saute till tender. Stir in remaining ingredients except macaroni. Cover and cook for 10 minutes. When pasta is done, drain well. Stir into other ingredients. Heat. Garnish if desired. Variations: - substitute or add other vegetables such as chopped sweet red shredded carrot to sauteed veggies; substitute 1 t basil and 1 t oregano for savory, thyme, and cayenne pepper.

Servings: 5

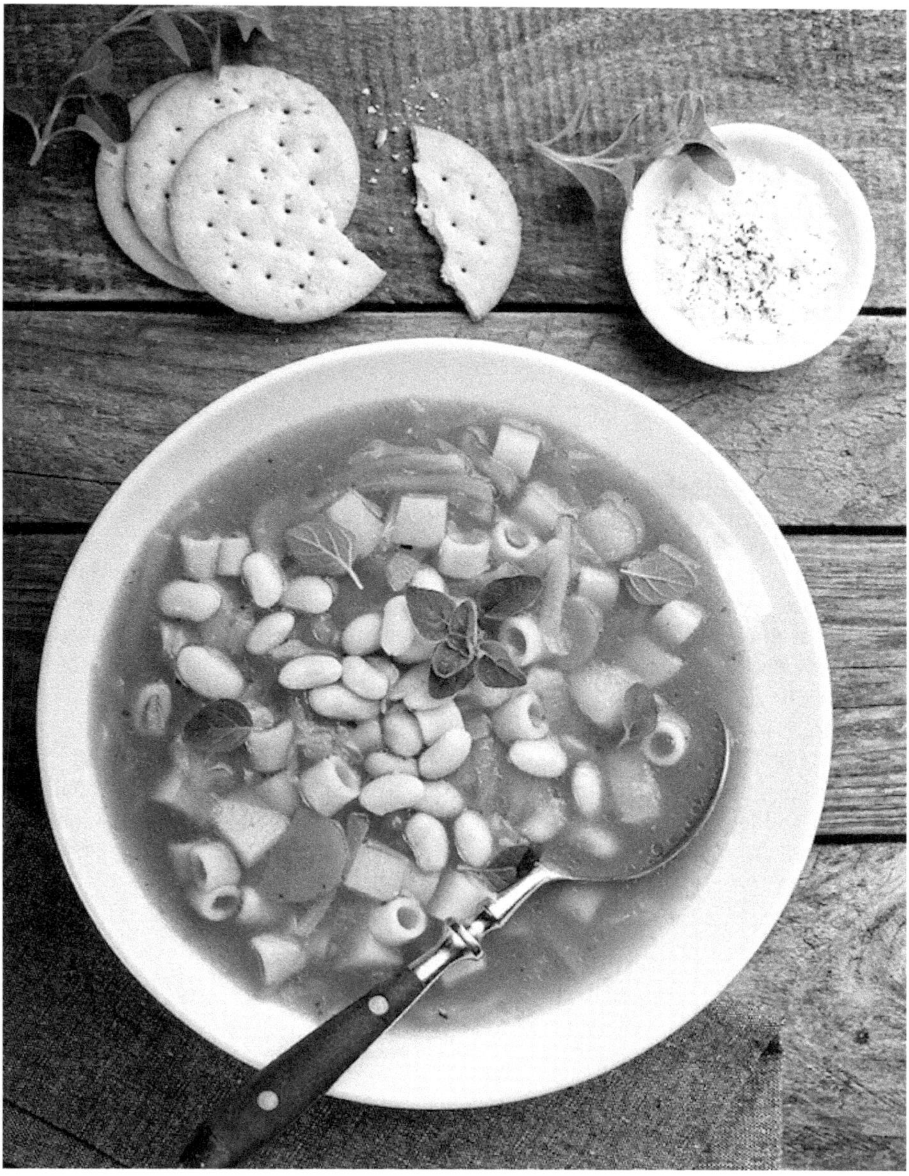

Pasta & Strawberries Romanoff

16	oz	Ronzoni pasta *
2	tsp	Walnut oil may substitute vegetable oil
2	pint	Fresh strawberries; sliced divided
2/3	cup	Toasted coconut **
1	cup	Heavy cream
4	Tbs	Confectioners sugar
4	tsp	Kirsh (cherry brandy); opt
1	tsp	Vanilla extract
1	cup	Walnut pieces; toasted**
		Salad greens

Procedure

1. * Use a tubular-type pasta such as mostaccioli or similar
2. Cook pasta according to package directions; drain. Rinse with cold water to cool quickly; drain well. In a large bowl, toss cooled pasta with oil; gently blend in 1-1/2 c strawberries and coconut. Set aside. In food processor or blender, process remaining strawberries and rest of ingredients except greens and walnuts until strawberries are pureed and mixture is slightly thickened. Serve pasta on greens. Spoon dressing over top; sprinkle with toasted walnuts.
3. ~ from Ronzoni Pasta Passion booklet ** TO TOAST WALNUTS/COCONUT: Conventional: Heat oven to 350 deg. F. Spread ingredients in a shallow baking dish; bake 8-10 minutes, stirring occasionally, until golden brown. Microwave: Spread walnuts and coconut on glass plate. Microwave on high 5-8 minutes or until lightly browned, stiring after each minute.

Servings: 6

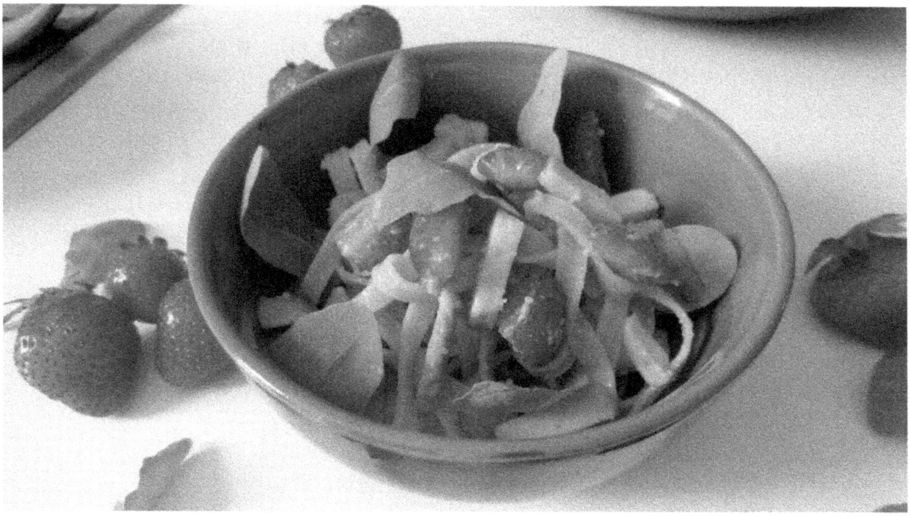

Pasta Al Forno

1	quantity tomato chipotle sauce	1	bunch fresh basil, chopped roughly
1	round mozzarella cheese, (c 100 g/4 oz.)	8 oz	dried pasta such as penne rigate or similar pasta
4 oz	Parmesan freshly grated		

Procedure

1. Preheat oven to 400F. Cook pasta in boiling water until slightly before al dente (it will cook further in the oven). Drain pasta and set aside.
2. Chop mozzarella finely and add to tomato sauce with 3/4 of grated parmesan and 3/4 of basil. Stir, cover and simmer for a few minutes more until cheese melts.
3. Mix pasta thoroughly with sauce, turn into oiled gratin or lasagna dish. Scatter remaining basil and parmesan over top. Bake in top part of oven for 15-20 minutes until browned on top. Serve with green salad and a good Chianti (e.g. Antinori) or Rosso di Montalcino (Il Poggione or Col D'Orcia).
4. Carnivores can also add sliced Italian pizza or luganega sausage (1/4 inch thick sliced on bias) to this when the cheeses are put into the sauce, brown the luganega slices in a little oil first. Spanish chorizo also works well.

Servings: 1

Recipe Type

Bbq List, Sides

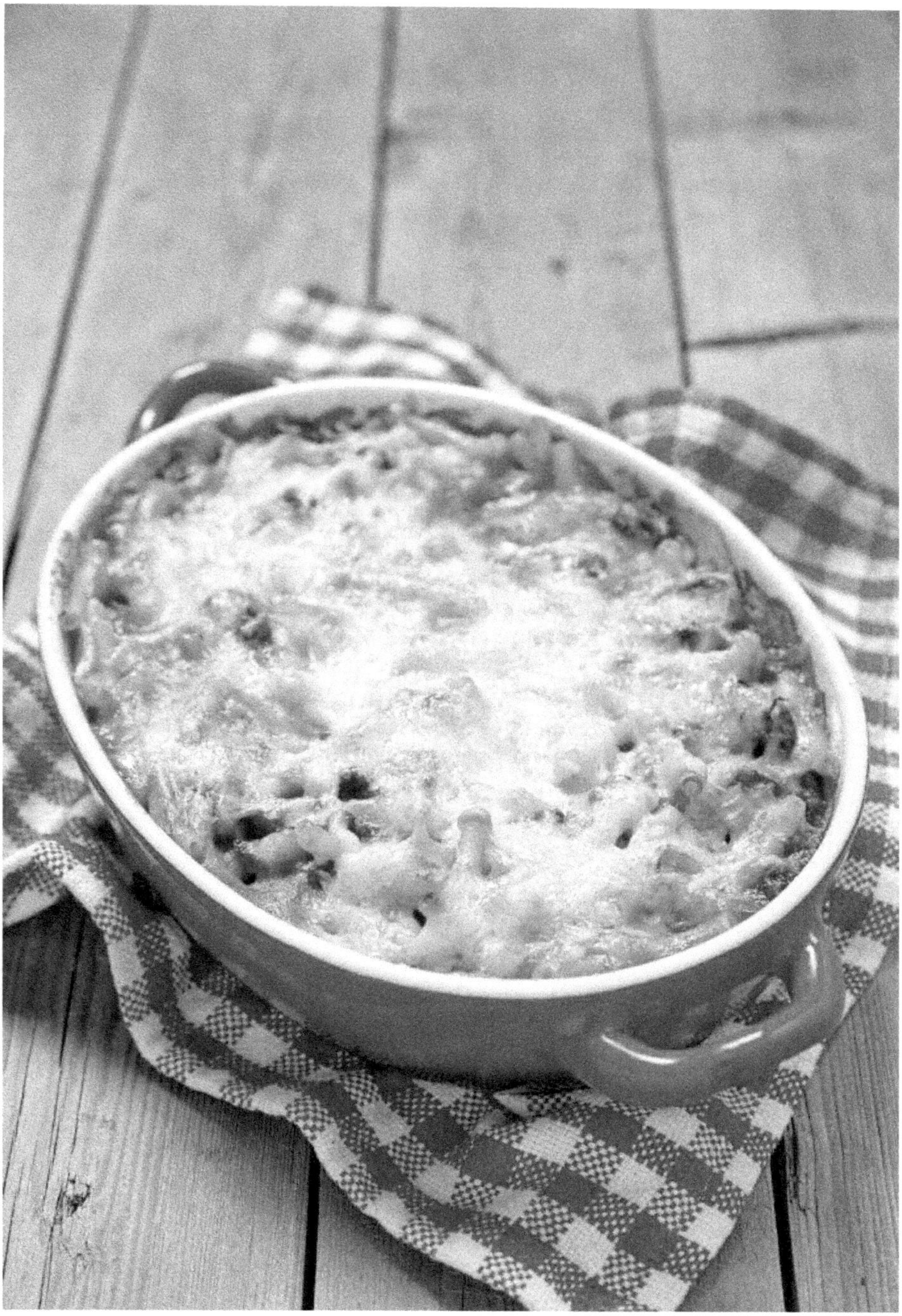

Pasta Al Pesto

8 oz	Pasta (preferably linguine)	3	x Sm Zucchini, thinly sliced
3	x Carrots, thinly sliced	1/4 lb	Peapods
2 Tbs	Safflower or Olive oil		

Procedure

1. ----PESTO---- c Fresh Basil Leaves /4 c Pine nuts (pignolli) x Cloves Garlic T Olive oil
2. PASTA GARNISH: freshly ground black pepper and Parmesan cheese, optional """""""""""""""""""""""""""""""""""""" ' PESTO: Place ingredients in bowl of food processor. Process until smooth, using rubber scraper to push down the sides occasionally. Makes 1/2 cup. Variations: - add 3/4 c freshly grated Parmesan Cheese - subst. cream cheese, kefir, or Neufchatel cheese for oil - subst. walnuts or hazelnuts for pine nuts PASTA: Boil a large pot of water; cook pasta until al dente. While pasta is cooking, prepare pesto; set aside, covered. Steam carrots. Meanwhile, in skillet, heat oil. Add zucchini and peapods. Stir continuously until crisp/tender. When pasta is done, drain well; toss pesto with noodles until they are well coated. Then toss in vegetables. Garnish with pepper and cheese. VARIATIONS: - add 1/2 c Parmesan cheese to Pesto - add or substitute other steamed or sauteed vegetables such as mushrooms, peas, or sweet red pepper.

Servings: 6

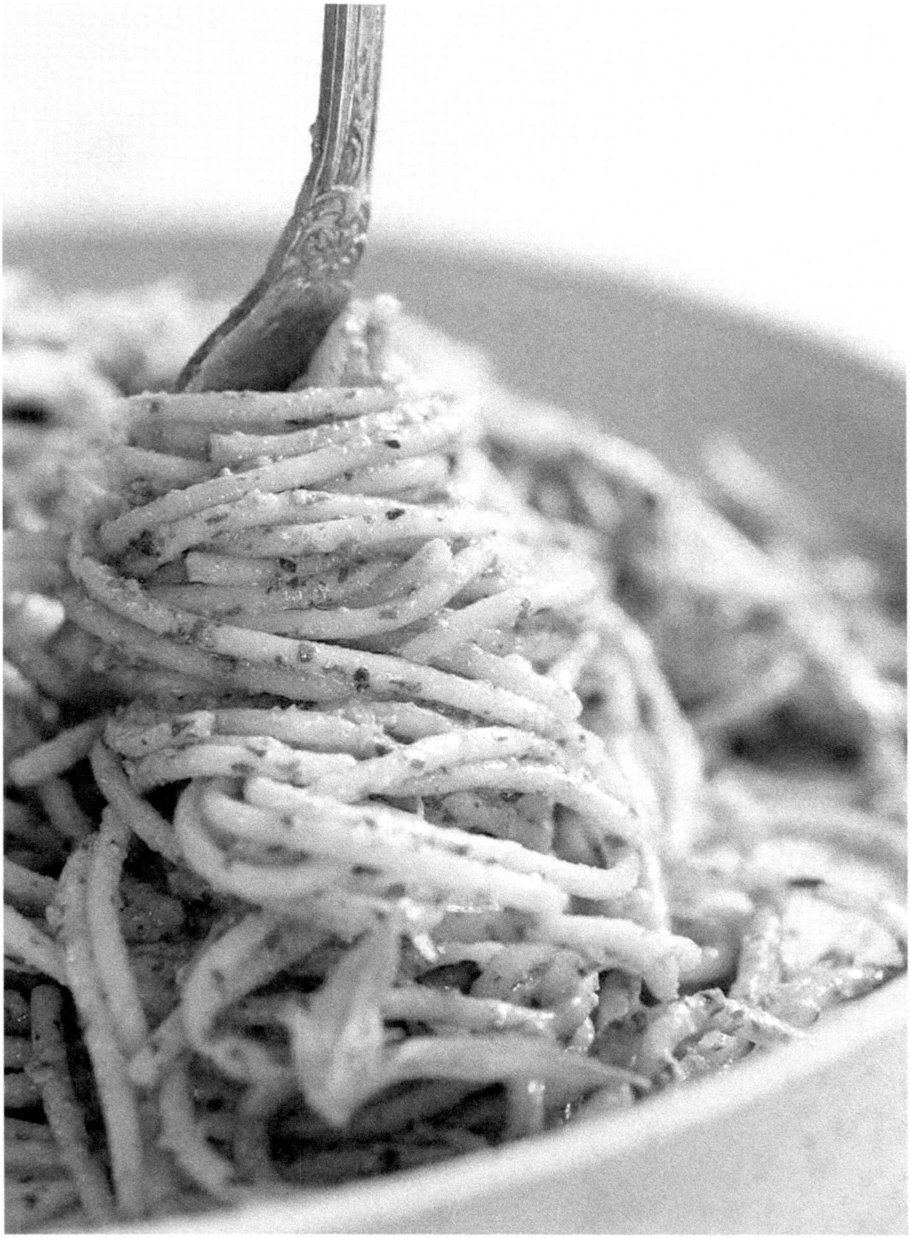

Pasta Ala Oglio with Shrimp

1	Tbs	Light margarine	1	tsp	Dill
1	tsp	Preminced garlic or	1	tsp	Parsley
2 1/2		Cloves of minced garlic	1/2	tsp	Basil
1	cup	Cooked pasta of your choice			Salt and pepper to taste
					Parmesan cheese to taste
3	oz	Cooked shrimp			

Procedure

1. In a small saute pan, saute the margarine and garlic. Note: the author likes garlic, you may choose to add more or less as you prefer.
2. Once the garlic and margarine have reached a tender consistency, add the spices, and blend. Add the cooked shrimp, and saute until shrimp is warm.
3. Add cooked pasta to saute pan, toss gently but thoroughly, and transfer to warm plate. Add salt, pepper, and parmesan cheese to taste.
4. Linda Fields
5. Each serving contains: 3 protein exchanges, 2 bread exchanges, 1 1/2 fat exchange

Servings: 1

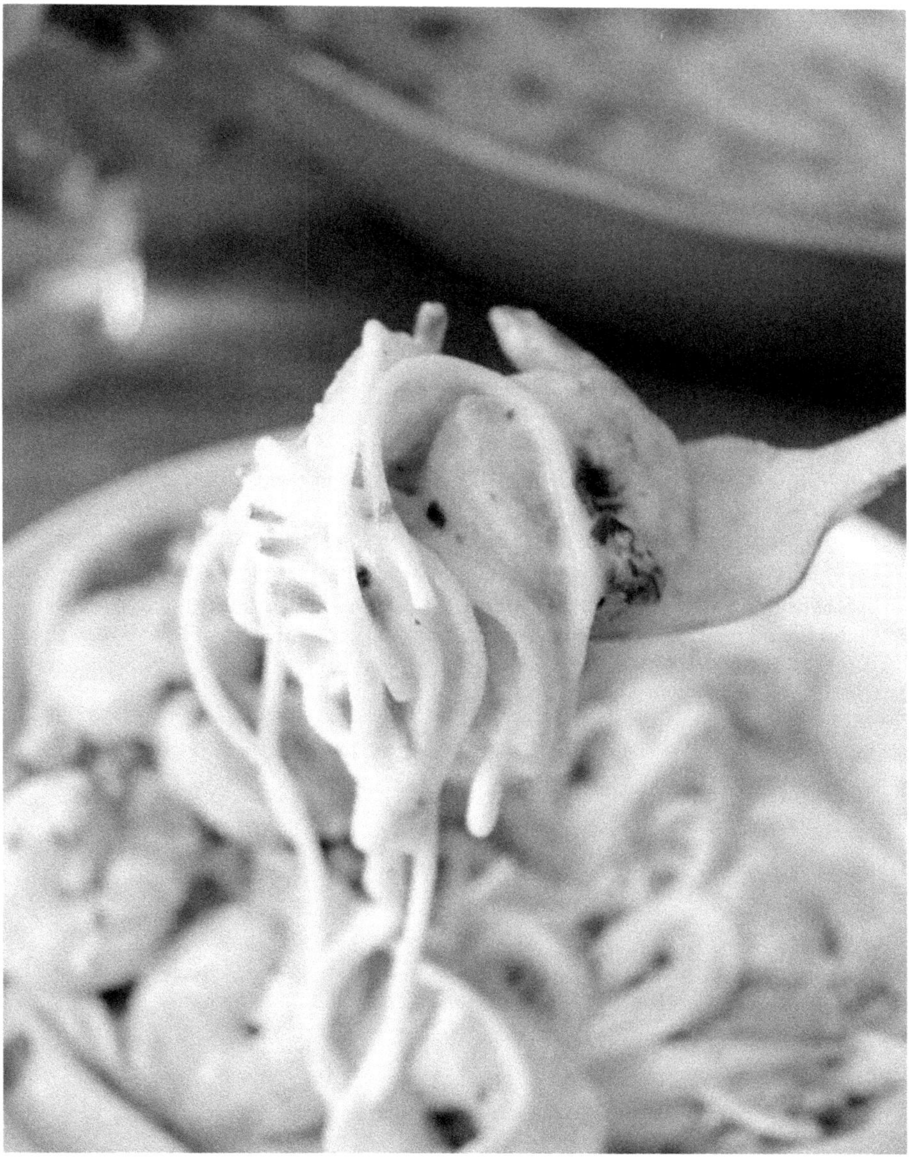

Pasta ala Puttanesca

1	lb	Spaghetti, linguini, or Other pasta of your choice	1/2	cup	Tiny black Nicoise olives
2		cn Peeled italian tomatoes	1/4	cup	Drained capers
1/4	cup	Olive oil	4		cl Garlic, peeled and minced
1	tsp	Oregano	8		Anchovie filets, chopped
1/8	tsp	Dried red pepper flakes	1/2	cup	Chopped parsley
			2	Tbs	Salt

Procedure

1. Bring 4 quarts water to a boil; add salt and stir in spaghetti. Cook until tender but still firm. Drain, and transfer to heated plates.
2. While spaghetti is cooking, drain the tomatoes, cut them cross-wise into halves, and squeeze out as much liquid as possible. Combine tomatoes and olive oil in a skillet and bring to a boil. Keep the sauce at a full boil and add remaining ingredients except pasta, one at a time, stirring frequently.
3. Reduce heat and continue to cook for a few minutes, or until sauce has thickened to your liking. Serve immediately over hot pasta and garnish with additional parsley.
4.

Servings: 4

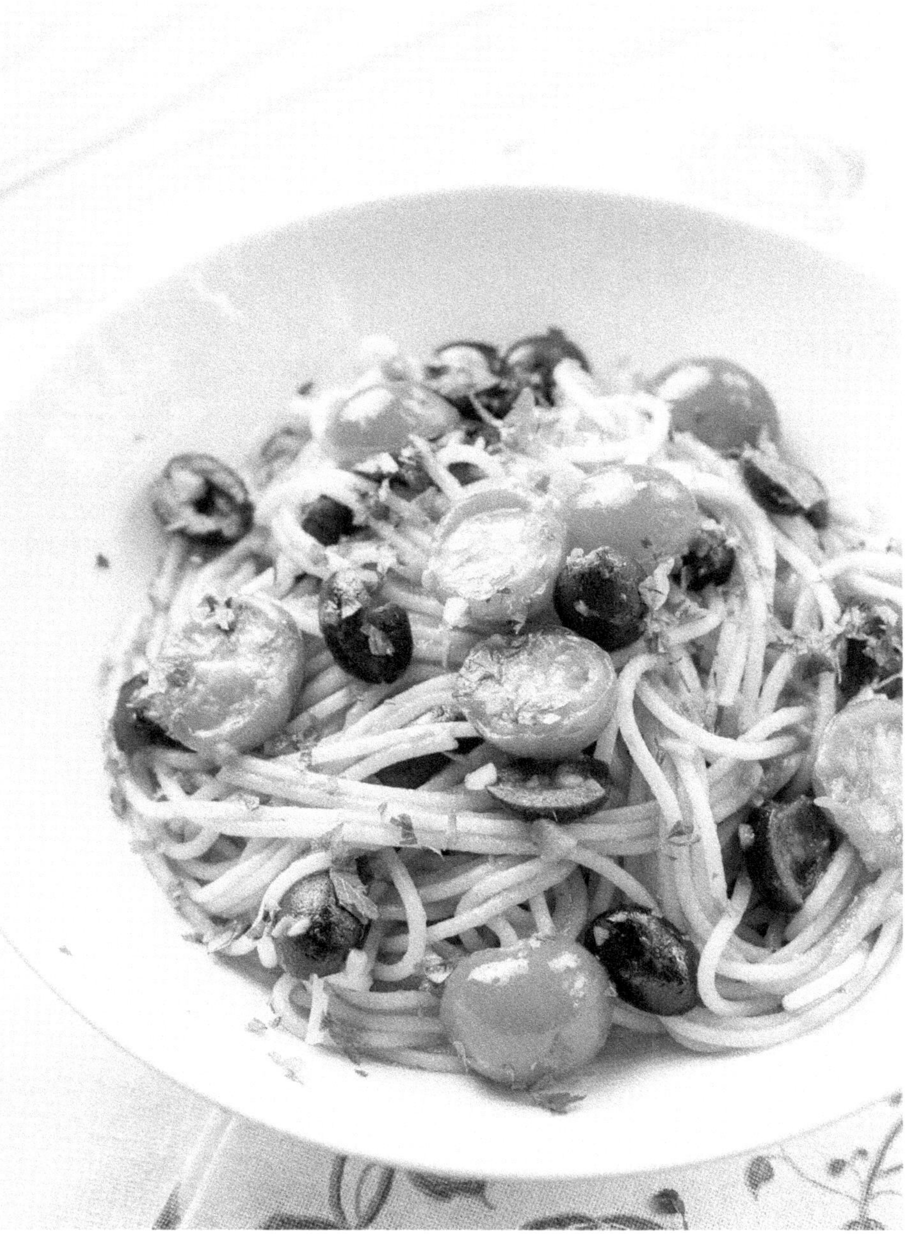

Pasta and Smoked Salmon Salad

3/4	lb	Smoked salmon cut in strips	1	cup	Whipping cream
1	quart	Water	3/4	cup	Dry white wine
3/4	lb	Linguini or spaghetti; dry	1	Tbs	Dijon mustard
2	Tbs	White vinegar	1/4	cup	Grated parmesan
1/2	cup	Onion; finely chopped	1/2	cup	Fresh parsley spriggs

Procedure

1. Bring water to boil, cook pasta until tender; drain.
2. As pasta cooks, boil venegar with onion in a frying pan over high heat until vinegar evaporates, about 2 minutes. Add cream, wine and mustard. Boil, uncovered, stirring often, until sauce is reduced to -3/4 cups. Add hot drained pasta; lift with forks to coat with sauce.
3. Divide pasta and sauce evenly amoung 4 dinner plates; sprinkle each with 1 tb parmesan. Arrange salmon beside each serving of pasta, garnish with parsley. Season with salt and pepper.

Servings: 4

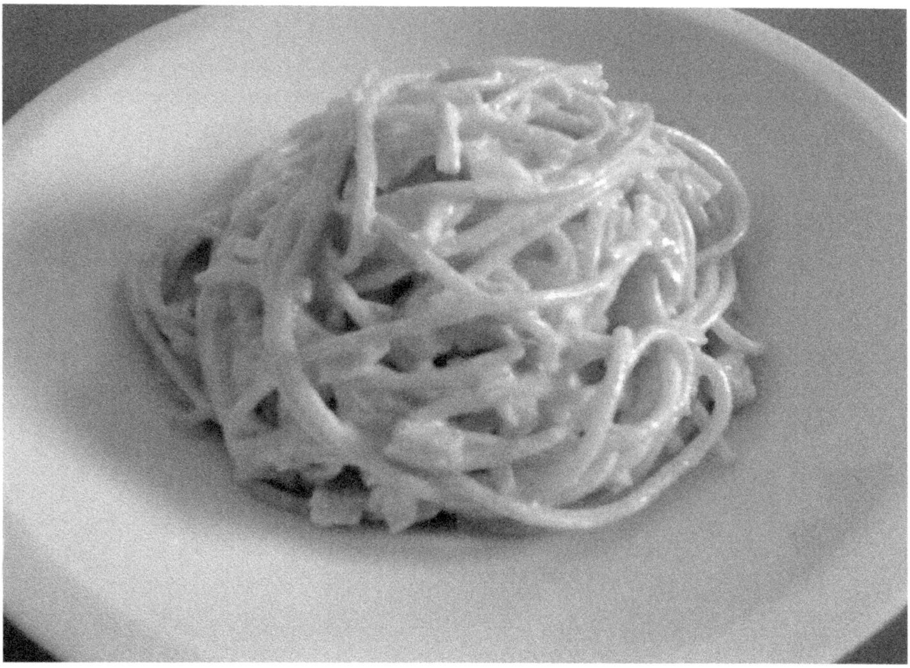

Pasta Carbonara

1	lb	Thick-sliced bacon, diced	1/3	cup	Chopped Italian parsley
2	Tbs	Salt			Grated Parmesan cheese
1	lb	Linguini			Fresh ground pepper to taste
3		Eggs			

Procedure

1. Saute the bacon in a small skillet until crisp. Remove with a slotted spoon and drain well on a paper towel.
2. Boil the water and cook linguini until firm and tender.
3. Meanwhile, beat the eggs thoroughly in a large bowl suitable for serving. Have the cooked bacon and the chopped parsley ready at hand.
4. When the pasta is done, drain it immediately in a colander, and pour into the bowl of eggs and immediately begin tossing it. As the strands of pasta become coated with the beaten eggs, their heat will cook the eggs.
5. Sprinkle the bacon and parsley on, and serve immediately. This is great with lots of freshly grated Parmesan cheese and freshly ground black pepper.
6.

Servings: 4

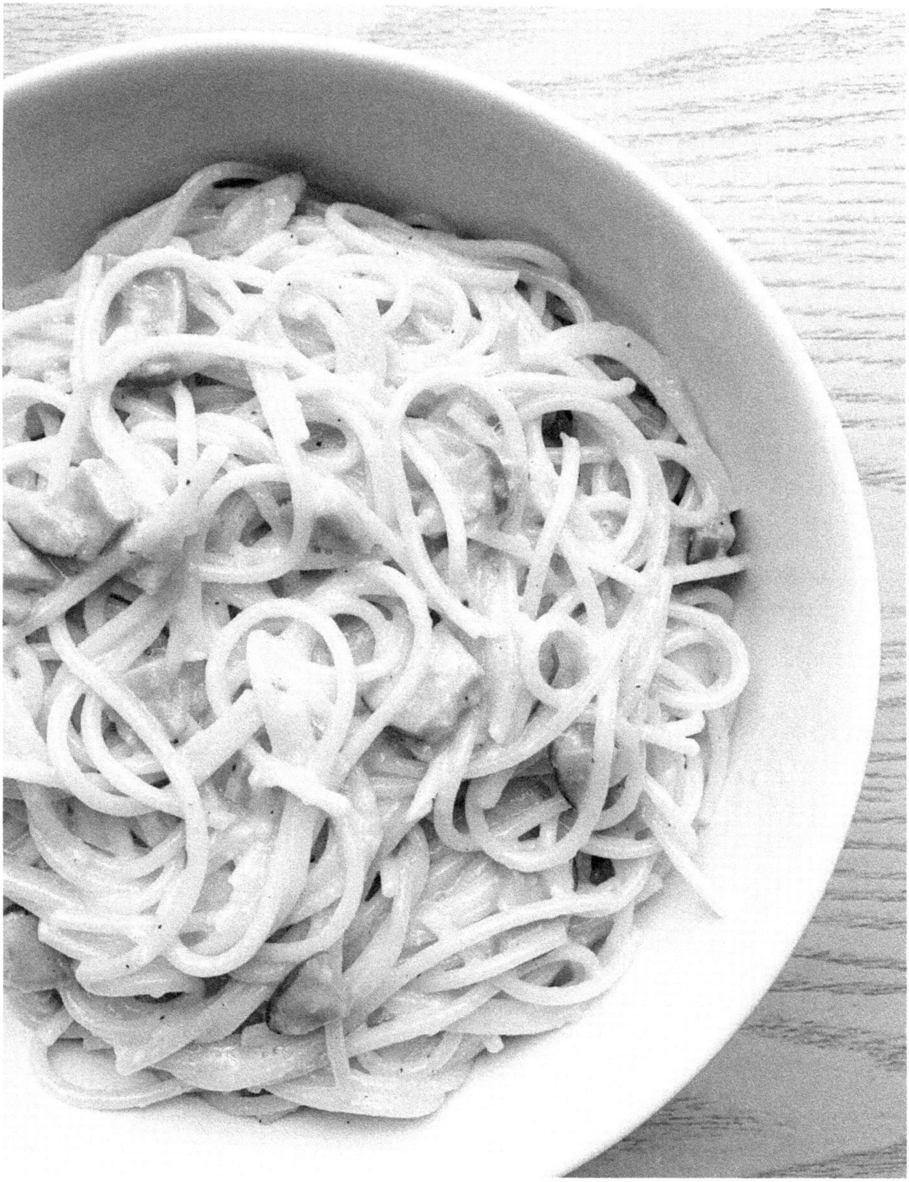

Pasta Chowder

2 cups	Small Shells, Ditalini or Stars, uncooked	
3 Tbs	margarine	
1	small onion, chopped	
1	clove garlic, minced	
4 cups	milk	
2 Tbs	chopped fresh parsley	
1 1/2 cups	shredded Cheddar cheese	
2	6 1/2-oz. cans minced clams, undrained	
	Salt to taste	
	Pepper to taste	

Procedure

1. Prepare pasta according to package directions; drain.
2. In large saucepan or Dutch oven, melt margarine. Add onion and garlic. Cook until tender.
3. Stir in remaining ingredients, except pasta. Cook over medium heat, stirring constantly, until soup is hot and cheese melts. Do not boil. Stir in pasta. Heat through.

Servings: 6

Recipe Type

Pasta, Soup

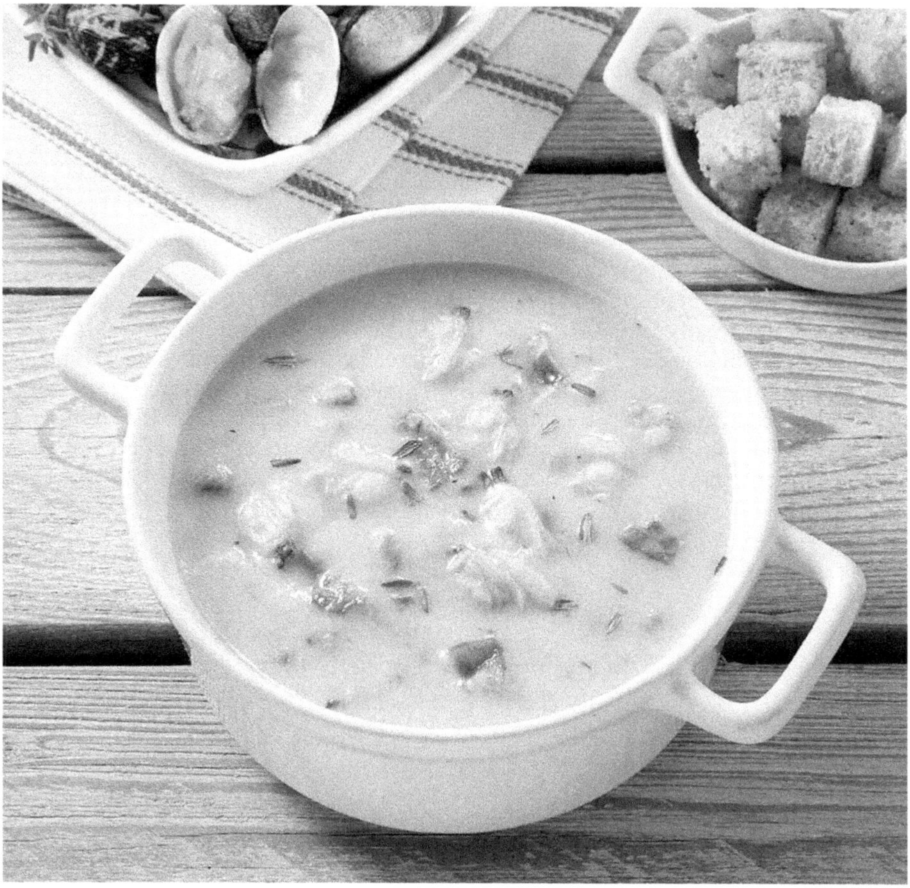

Pasta Di Pina

3	Tbs	Olive Oil	3 1/2	cup	Water
4		Med. Cloves Garlic *	6	oz	Uncooked Fine Egg Noodles
2	Tbs	Fresh Bread Crumbs			
1/8	tsp	Pepper	2	Tbs	Finely Chopped Parsley
1		Env. Golden Onion Soup Mix	1	x	Grated Parmesan Cheese

Procedure

1 * Garlic cloves should be finely chopped. In medium skillet, heat oil and cook garlic with bread crumbs over medium heat, stirring constantly, until garlic and bread crumbs are golden. Stir in pepper; set aside. In large saucepan, thoroughly blend golden onion recipe soup mix with water. Bring to a boil, then stir in uncooked noodles. Simmer uncovered stirring frequently, 7 minutes or until noodles are tender. (DO NOT DRAIN!) remove from heat, then toss with bread crumb mixture and parsley. Sprinkle with cheese and serve. Makes about 4 appetizer or 2 main-dish servings.

Servings: 4

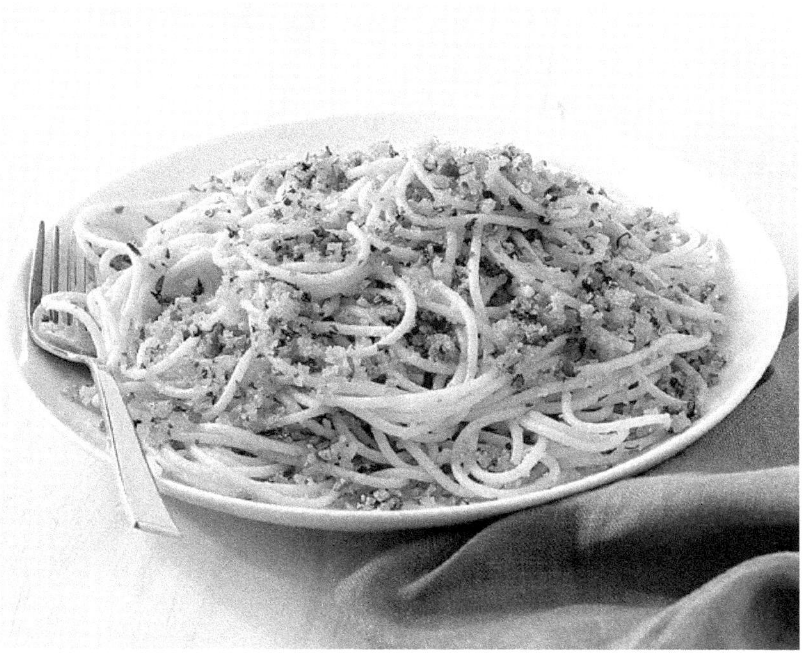

Pasta E Fagiole Soup for Crockpot

	Olive oil	1 cup	Elbow macaroni; cooked
1	lg Omion; chopped	1	lg Can tomatoes
1	cn White kidney beans; drained		Grated cheese; to taste
5	Garlic cloves; chopped		Chopped parsley; to taste
2	cn Chicken broth		Salt and pepper; to taste

Procedure

1 Saute the onion and garlic in olive oil for a few minutes. Chop up or lightly process the tomatoes and place into a crockpot along with the broth and sauteed onion and garlic. Add the parsley and a little salt and pepper, cook for about 3 hours on LOW. Then and only then add the cooked macaroni and beans. Serve with a bit of grated cheese if desired. NOTE: If fresh garden tomatoes are available, remove skins of 6 or 7 and use them instead of canned tomatoes. Oh Mama Mia!

Servings: 4

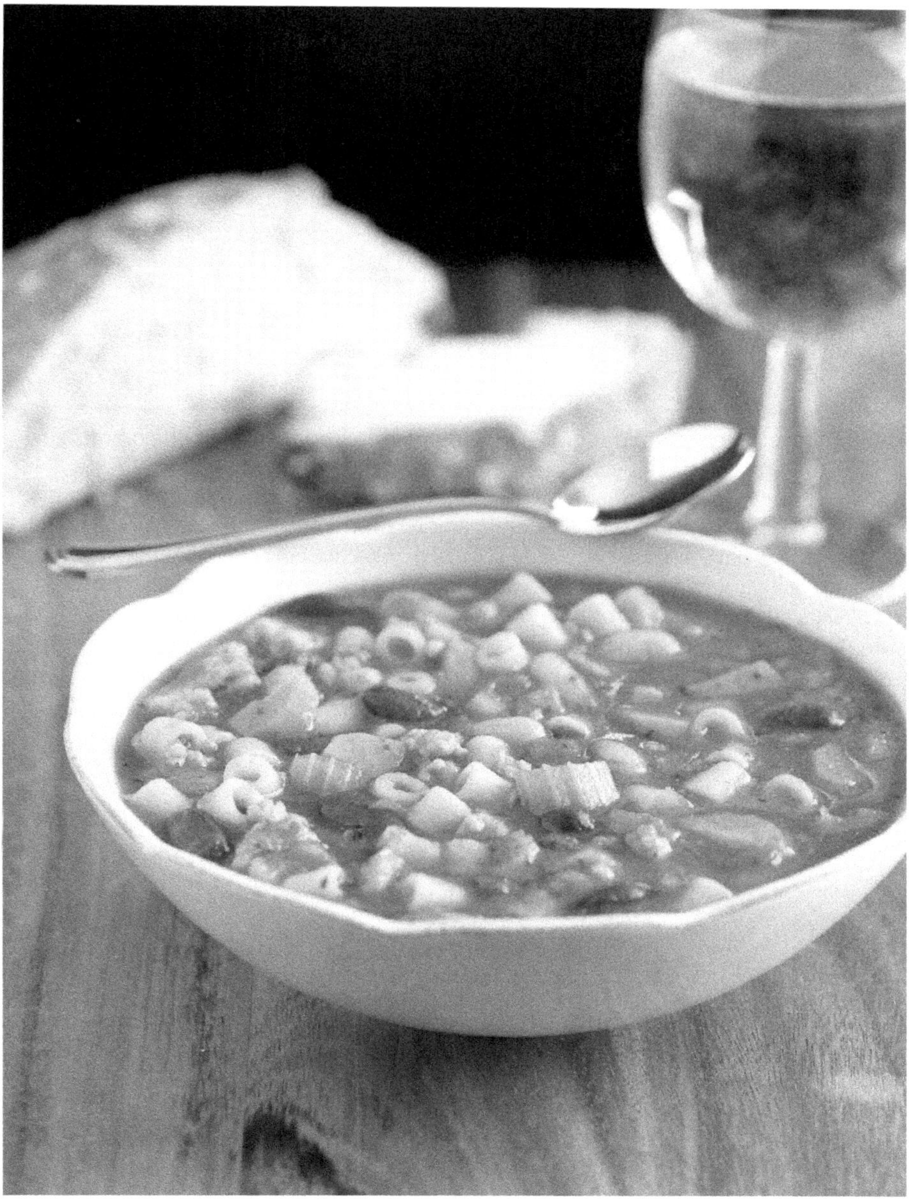

Pasta E Fagioli

		BATTUTO==	4		Peeled plum tomatoes
2		Slices lean salt pork	2	quart	Hot water
1		sm Onion	2	tsp	Salt
1		md Garlic clove	2	cup	Cooked shell beans
1		Celery stalk	2	cup	Small pasta
3	Tbs	Olive oil	4	Tbs	Grated Romano or Parmesan
		SOUP==			

Procedure

1 Put the slices of salt pork on a chopping board. Top them with the onion, garlic and celery and chop, then mince until the pile has turned to a paste. Put the battuto in a big soup pot with the olive oil over medium heat. Saute until golden, then add the tomatoes and cook again for about 3 minutes, or until the tomatoes have blended a bit and softened. Add the hot water, salt and beans, and bring to a good boil. Once the beans are heated through, crush a few beans against the side of the pot, add the pasta and continue cooking until it is well done. By this time the soup is really so thick you may want to add a little more water. Taste for salt, and add some if necessary. Serve with a sprinkling of the cheese.

Servings: 6

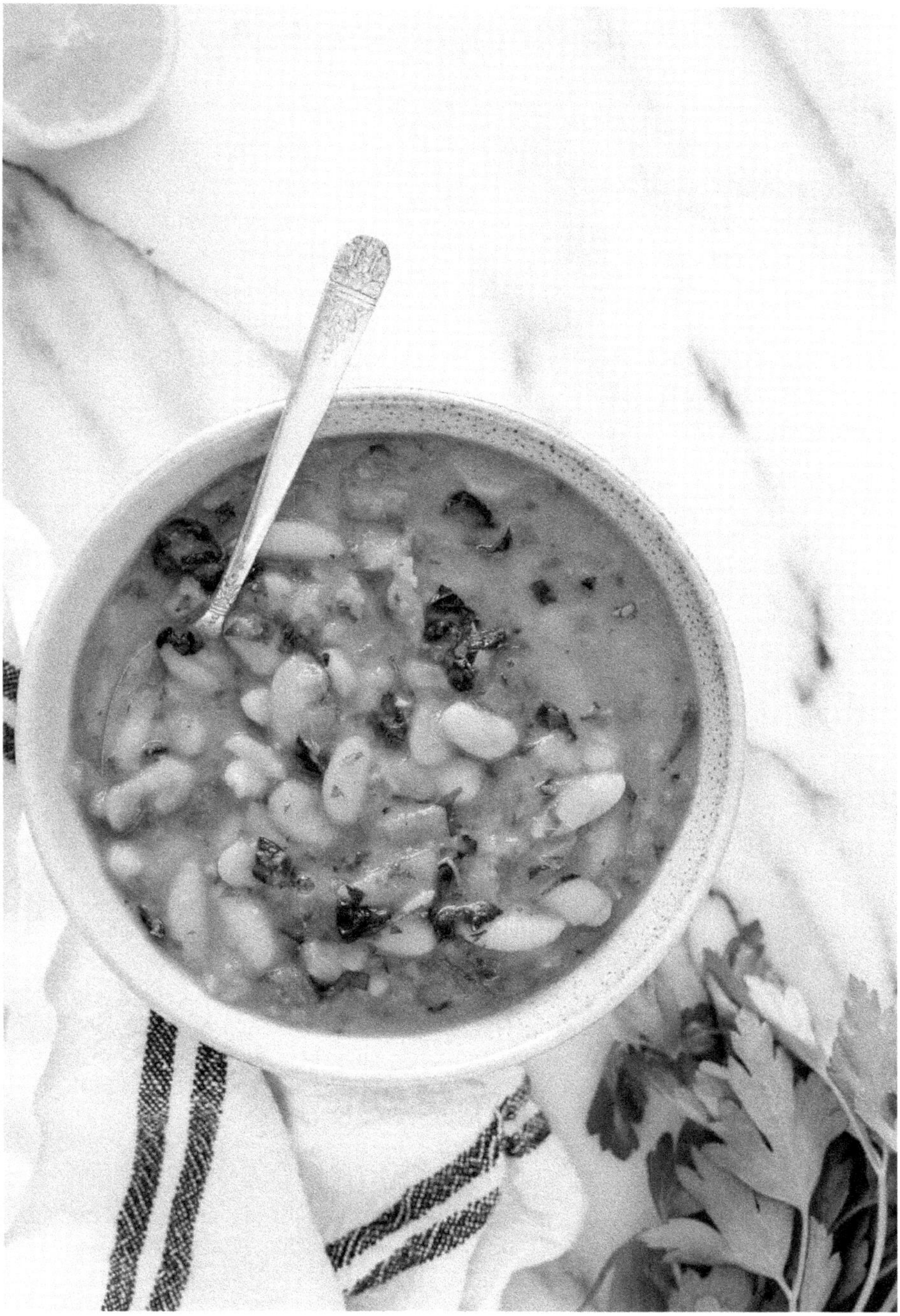

Pasta Flora, Athens Style

1/2	lb	Sweet butter	4		Dried figs
1/2	cup	Granulated sugar	1/3	cup	Raisins
2		Eggs	1		Orange (grated rind only)
6	Tbs	Cognac	1	cup	Apricot jam
2	cup	All-purpose flour (or more)	1	Tbs	Lemon juice (optional)
1/4	tsp	Salt	2	tsp	Cornstarch
1/2	tsp	Baking powder	1/3	cup	Orange juice
2	cup	Stewed apricots			

Procedure

1. Using an electric mixer, beat the butter until light and fluffy and gradually add the sugar, 1 egg and an egg yolk, and 3 tablespoons of the Cognac, beating thoroughly after each addition. Sift 2 cups of the flour with the salt and baking powder and add slowly to the batter, while beating on medium speed. Remove the beaters and finish by hand, adding only enough flour to make a soft dough. Knead. Cover and refrigerate for at least 30 minutes.
2. Meanwhile, slice the apricots into uniform pieces and place in an enameled pan. Soak the figs and raisins in the remaining Cognac until swollen, then mince and add to the apricots along with the orange rind, jam, and lemon juice and stir into the apricot mixture, then cook over medium heat until thick, stirring constantly with a wooden spoon. Cool.
3. Remove the dough from the refrigerator and set aside about one-third for the latticed top. Using your fingers (the dough will be too soft to roll), press the larger portion of dough into a buttered 9 x 2-inch baking pan, pressing evenly about 1/4-inch up the sides. Pour the filling into the dough-lined pan.
4. Divide the remaining dough into walnut-sized balls and roll each ball into 1/2-inch strips. Using the strips, make a lattice over the top of the pastry. If using a glaze, beat the remaining egg white slightly with a fork and brush on the dough stips. Bake in a moderate oven (350 F) for 45 minutes, or until golden in color. Remove and cool in the pan on a rack.
5. To serve, cut into 1-1/2-inch (or smaller) squares with a sharp knife.
6. Note: You may prefer to use peaches and peach jam, strawberries and strawberry jam, and so on, instead of apricots; also diced candied peel adds a colorful note when substituting for figs; and slivered almonds may be added to the filling.

Servings: 36

Pasta Green Salad

FOR THE SALAD

3	cup	Cooked and cooled rotini
2	cup	Shredded Swiss cheese
1		package 10 oz frozen cut green beans .thawed and drained
1		package 10 oz frozen green peas, .thawed and drained
1	cup	Green pepper strips cut in .half
1/2	cup	Sliced scallions
1	cup	Chopped cucumber

Procedure

1. --FOR THE DRESSING-- /3 c Mayonnaise /3 c Plain yogurt tb Grated parmesan cheese tb Lemon juice /2 ts Dried dill ts Sugar /4 ts Salt /4 ts Pepper
2. In a small bowl, combine all the dressing ingredients. Mix until well-blended; set aside. If not serving immediately, cover and chill until ready to use.
3. Place the cooled rotini in a large bowl and toss with the remaining ingredients, except the dressing. Cover and chill until ready to use. Just before serving, mix the dressing again and toss into the salad.
4.
5. Note: This is a really simple throw-together dressing that works well with other seasonings, fresh herbs, lime juice instead of lemon, and even lowfat mayonnaise and yogurt, too. You can enjoy this creamy dressing as above for a hearty summer meal, or simply serve it as a smooth dressing for your tossed green salad.

Servings: 6

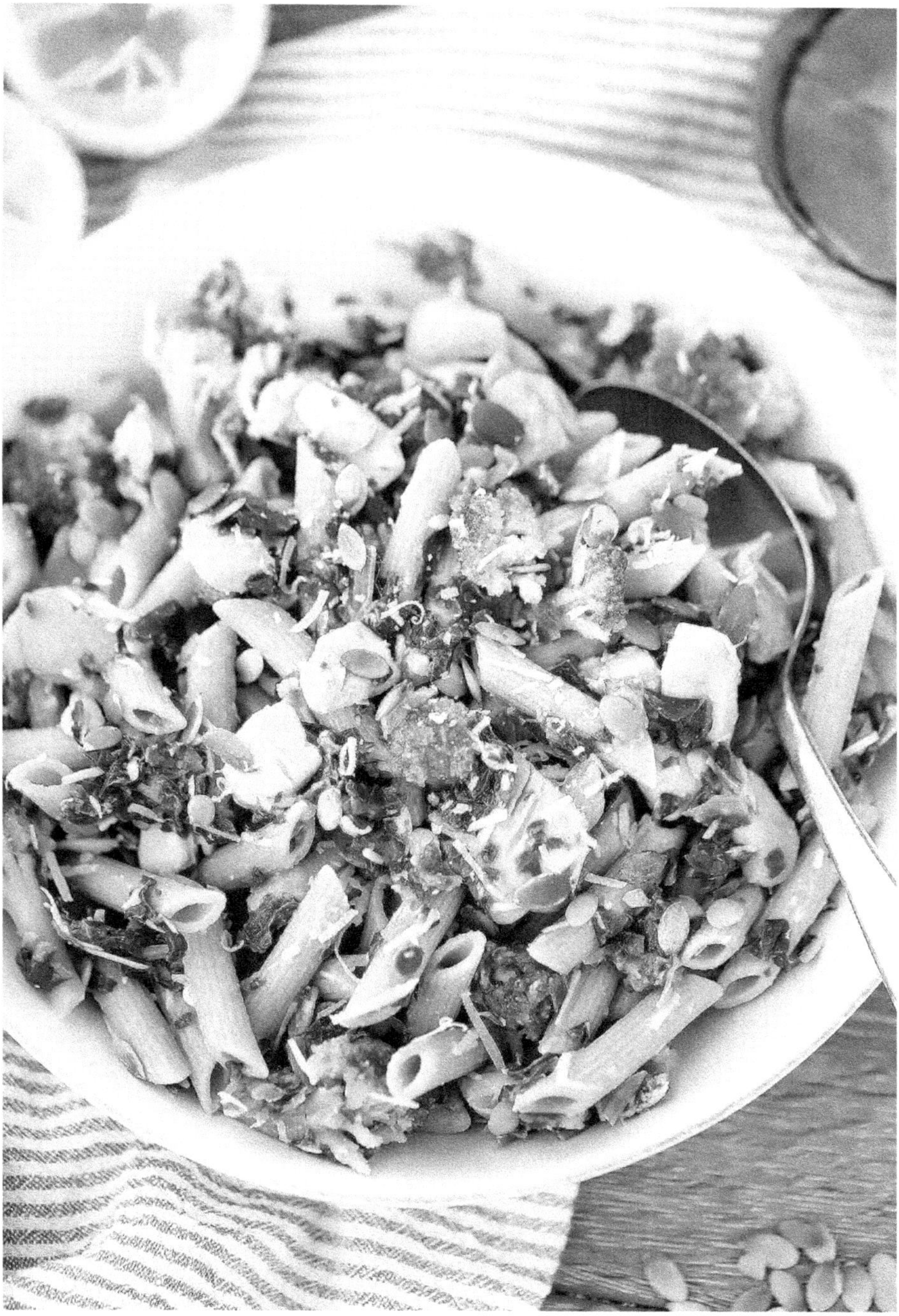

Pasta in Cream Sauce w/Poultry Magic

1/3 lb	Spaghetti or rotini	2 tsp	Poultry Magic or Piz & past.
6	Tbs Margarine or unsalted butter	2 cup	Half & Half or heavy cream
1/4 cup	Finely chopped green onions		

Procedure

1 Cook the spaghetti accordint to package just to al dente stage; immediately drain and rinse with hot watedr to wash off starch, then with cold water to stop the cooking process; drain again. (To prevent the pasta from sticking together, pour a very small amount of oil in the palm of your hand and rub through the pasta after rinsing.) In a large skillet melt the margarine over medium heat. Add the Magic Seasoning blend and saute about 1 minute to bring out the flavors, stirring occasionally; add the green onions and saute 1 to 2 minutes, continuing to stir. Gradually add the cream, either stirring or shaking the pan in a back and forth motion until the mixture reaches a boil. Simmer over medium heat until the sauce thickens somewhat, continuint to shake the pan, about 2 to 3 minutes. Add the ooked spaghetti; toss and stir until spaghetti is heated through, about 2 minutes. Pasta should swim in the sauce. Serve immediately and enjoy!

Servings: 4

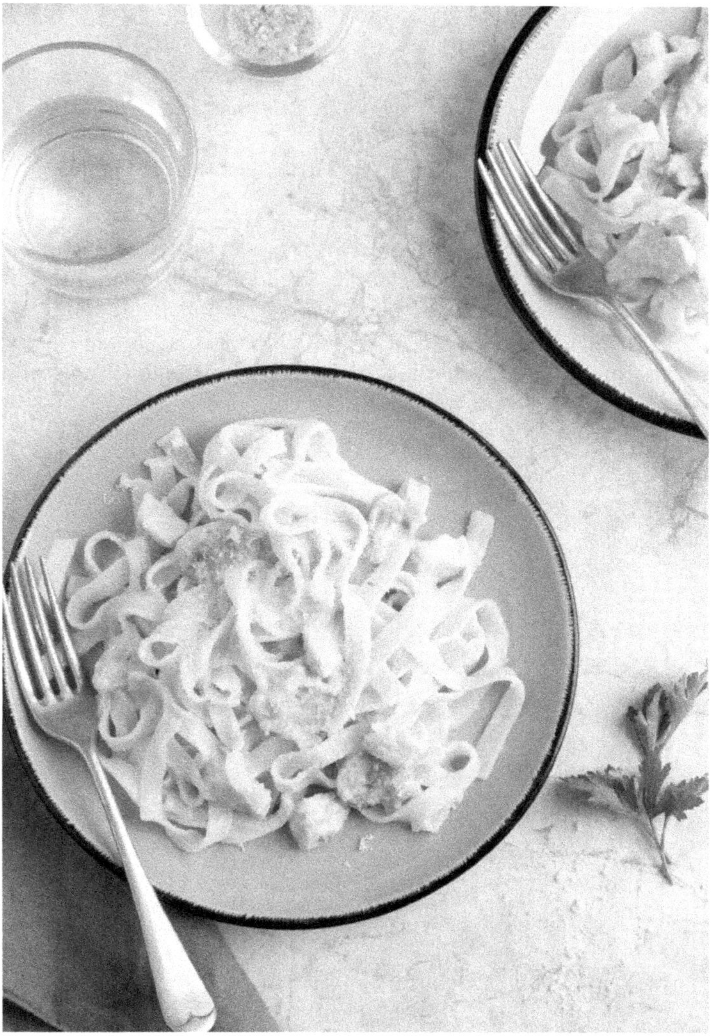

Pasta Marco Polo

PASTA & CHICKEN
Nonstick cooking spray
2 Tbs Sesame oil
1/2 lb Chicken breast, sliced
4 Scallions, sliced
12 oz Spicy Sesame Linguine

Procedure

1. ----SAUCE---- /2 c Chicken broth tb Soy sauce tb Sherry tb Sugar tb Cornstarch /2 tb Chili sauce /2 ts Garlic powder tb Hoisin sauce tb Minced ginger /2 ts Salt
2. Combine sauce ingredients. Spray skillet with nonstick cooking spray. Add oil & heat. Stir fry chicken until it begins to lose raw color. Add scallions. Add sauce. Add cooked pasta and stir until blended.

Servings: 6

Pasta Primavera

1/4	cup	Water	12	oz	Can Evaporated Skim Milk
2	cup	Sliced fresh Mushrooms	4	tsp	Cornstarch
9	oz	Pk French-style Green Beans	1/2	cup	Shredded Provolone *
			5	oz	Macaroni or fettucine
1/2	cup	Coarsely chopped Green Peppe	1		x Med Tomato, cut in wedges
1		x Clove garlic			

Procedure

1 * or Mozzarella cheese (2 oz) Cook pasta according to package directions; drain well. Meanwhile, for sauce, in a med saucepan combine water, mushrooms, frozen green beans, green or red pepper, garlic, 1/4 t salt, and 1/4 t pepper. Bring to boiling; reduce heat. Cover and simmer 4 minutes or till veggies are tender. Do not drain. Stir together milk and cornstarch; stir into vegetable mixture. Cook and stir over med heat till thickened and bubbly. Cook and stir for 1 minute more. Stir in cheese till melted. To serve, pour the sauce over pasta. Garnish with tomato wedges. Per serving: 297 calories, 17 g protein, 48 g carbohydrates, 5 g fat, mg cholesterol, 375 cholesterol, 375 mg sodium, 686 mg potassium.

Servings: 4

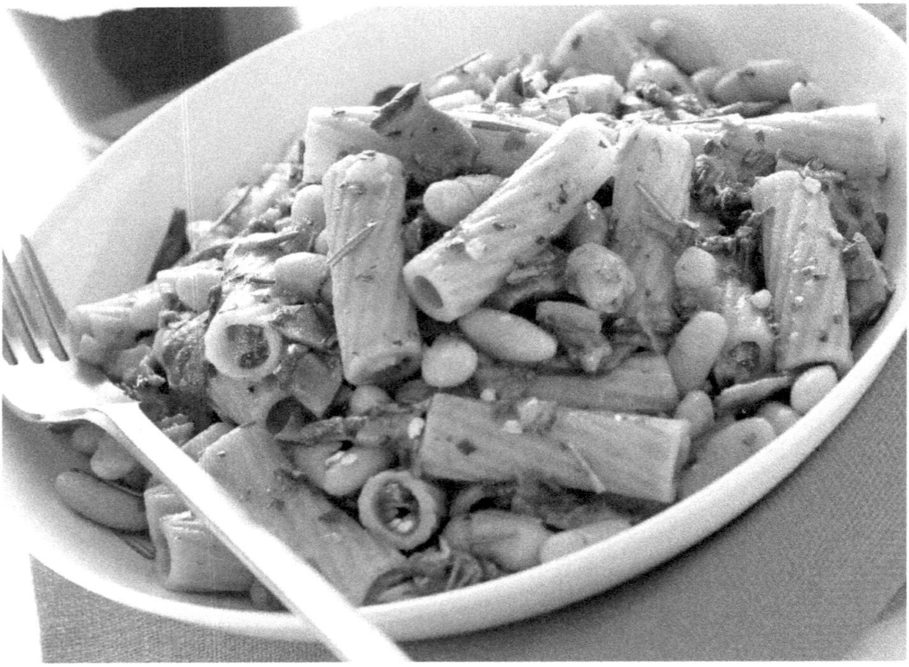

Pasta Primavera Special

1/2	cup	Salted butter	2/3	cup	(tl)carrots, zucchini, broc.
3	cup	35% cream	1		Enough fettuccine for 4
2	tsp	Fresh black pepper	2		Egg yolks
1/2	cup	Tomato sauce	2	Tbs	Cream

Procedure

1. Melt the butter in a large sauce pan. Add the cream and the pepper. Bring to a simmer. Add the tomato sauce and the precooked vegetables. Stir in the cooked pasta. Remember to cook it al dente still slightly firm to the bite. Whip the egg yolks with a fork and mix them into the cream. Whisk the mixture into the cream sauce and pasta. This will serve as a thickner. Make sure the pasta is completely coated with the sauce and serve with some parmesan cheese.

Servings: 4

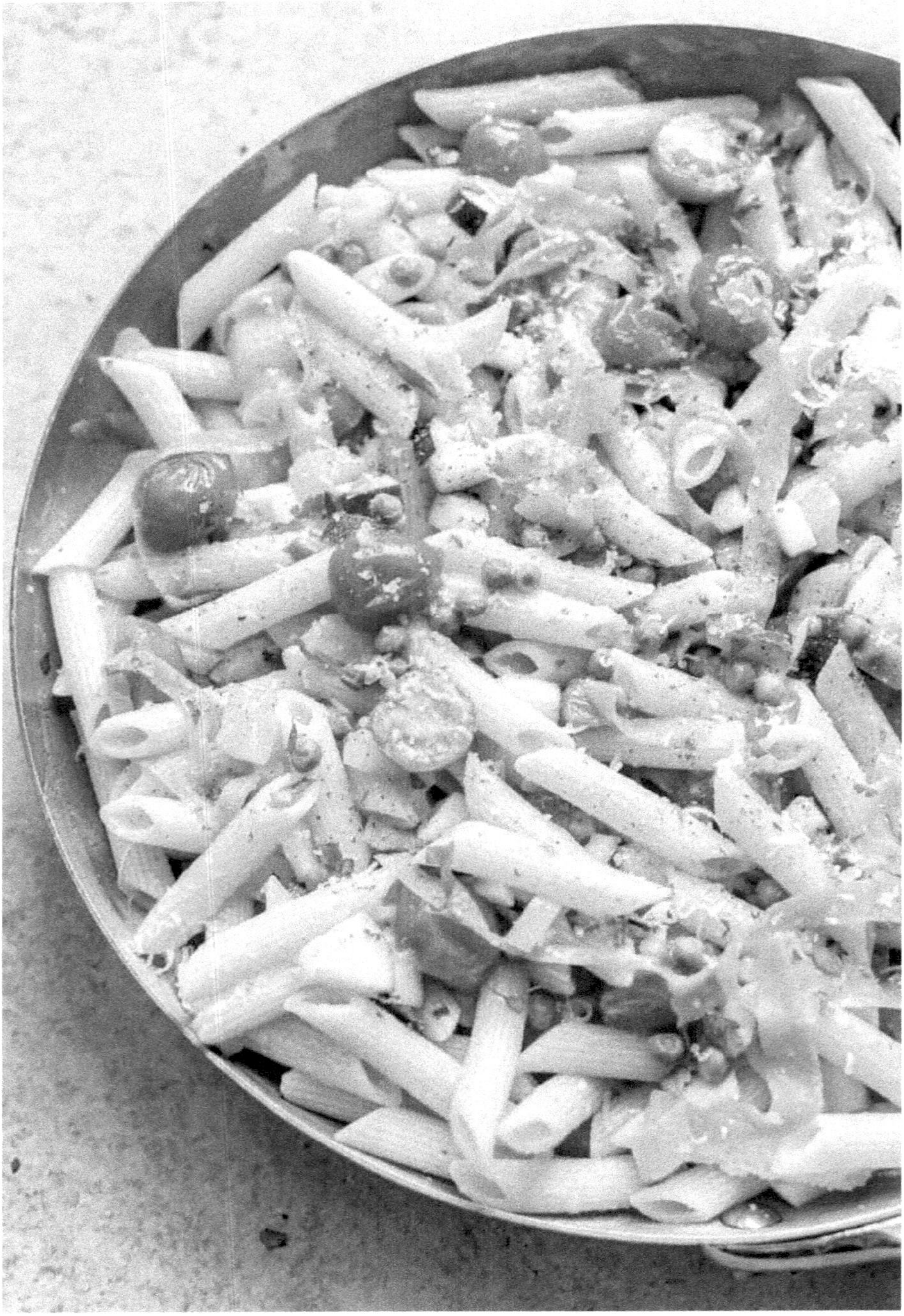

Pasta Salad

2/3 cup Rotini noodles	2 Tbs Mayonnaise
1/2 cup Frozen mixed vegetables	1 Tbs Chopped basil or parsley
1/4 cup Grated mozzarella cheese	1/2 tsp Dried oregano

Procedure

1 Cook pasta in a pot of boiling salted water until tender. Drain and rinse with cold water. Drain well. Add vegetables and cheese. Stir in mayonnaise, basil or parsley and oregano.

Servings: 2

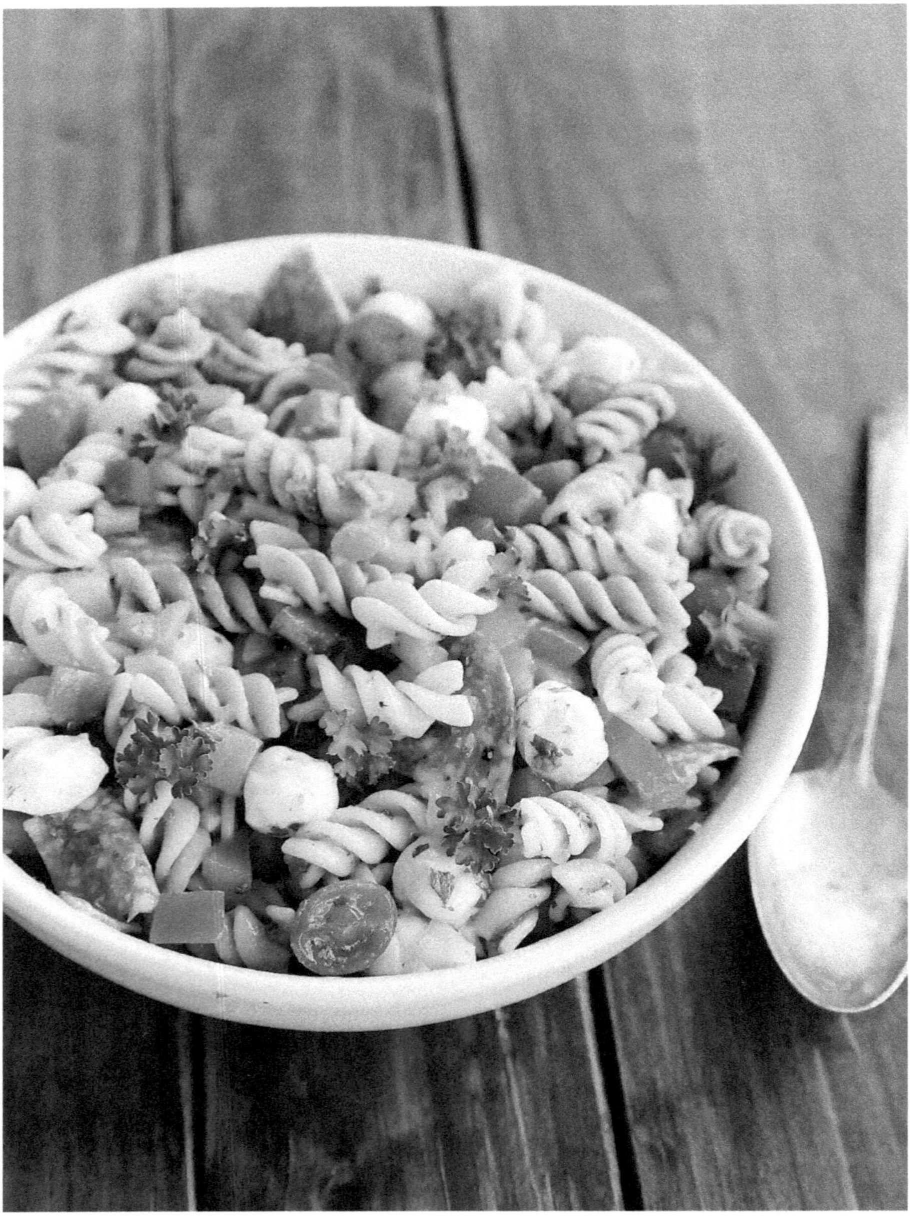

CONCLUSION

If you love pasta, you need this book.
If you love pasta, it's a must-have!

These recipes will make your mouth water, this book is a treasure. The recipes are easy, the ingredients are easy to find, and the Pasta masterpieces presented are incredibly quick to make.

Some of my favorites are the slightly sweeter pasta dishes slightly sweeter. Of course, there is plenty for spicy and savory lovers as well.
Delicious for restaurants, and all so easy to make on your own.

This book will also give you inspiration to experiment with different ingredients, as you'll find the extensive index extremely helpful.

Each recipe is truly superb, wonderfully easy to put together, and you won't have to make or buy a ton of toppings before you get started - just open the book and get started right away.

For family, friends, or creative indulgence, this book is your ultimate reference guide to great comfort food for all seasons. Enjoy!

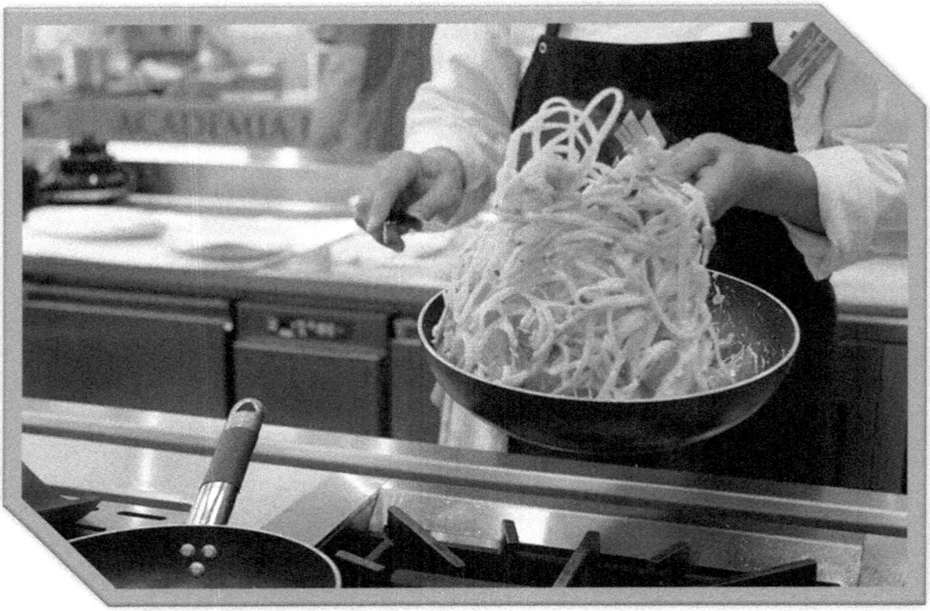